# THE ULTIMATE NORTH CAROLINA QUIZ BOOK

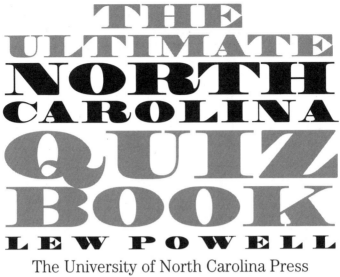

# THE ULTIMATE NORTH CAROLINA QUIZ BOOK

## LEW POWELL

The University of North Carolina Press

Chapel Hill and London

© 1999

The University of North Carolina Press

All rights reserved

Set in Century Light and Madrone by

Tseng Information Systems

Manufactured in the United States of America

The paper in this book meets the guidelines for

permanence and durability of the Committee on

Production Guidelines for Book Longevity of the

Council on Library Resources.

Library of Congress Cataloging-in-Publication Data

Powell, Lew.

The ultimate North Carolina quiz book / Lew Powell.

p.   cm.

ISBN 0-8078-4825-5 (pbk.: alk. paper)

1. North Carolina Miscellanea. 2. Questions and answers.

I. Title.

F254.6.P69   1999

975.6 – dc21   99-30994

CIP


03   02   01   00   99      5   4   3   2   1

*For Taylor*

# CONTENTS

# PREFACE

So you think you know North Carolina? I've lived here since 1974, and I don't begin to. This traditionally modest state – this "vale of humility between two mountains of conceit" – is rich in idiosyncrasy, from the Lost Colony to Biltmore House, from livermush to Cheerwine, from the Uwharries to the Great Dismal, from Aunt Bee to Little Eva.

It's rare week that I haven't stumbled onto at least one nugget of North Caroliniana. Do you know what future rock star paid an unwelcome visit to Carl Sandburg at his home in Flat Rock? What now-standard menu item at barbecue joints was borrowed from fish camps? What former heavyweight champion died in Raleigh? What county's population has the highest percentage of "Yankees"? What U.S. senator was born in North Wilkesboro? What town is named for a member of the Baseball Hall of Fame?

You'll find the answers to these questions – and some five hundred more – in *The Ultimate North Carolina Quiz Book*.

# THE ENVIRONS

*Of all the lonely, God-forsaken looking places
I ever saw, this Hatteras island takes the pre-
mium. It is simply a sandbar rising a little above
the water. . . . I don't think there is a bird or any
kind of animal, unless it is a dog, on the island,
not even a grasshopper, as one would have to
prospect the whole island to find a blade of grass,
and in the event of his finding one would sing
himself to death.*

*Private D. L. Day, Company B,
25th Massachusetts Volunteer Infantry,
writing in his diary at Hatteras Inlet in 1862*


*The ugliest collection of third-rate buildings in
America.*

*New York architect Robert A. M. Stern,
host of PBS's* Pride of Place *series, finding
little to his taste during a 1986 tour of
downtown Charlotte*

# QUESTIONS

**1**

An airplane takes off from the Raleigh-Durham International Airport and flies due south. Two thousand miles later, the pilot looks down and sees which one of the following: Cuba, the Gulf of Mexico, Brazil, or the Pacific Ocean?

**2**

North Carolina's first legislation on the automobile, enacted in 1907, stipulated what maximum speed on the open road?

**3**

True or false: Snow has been recorded on Mount Mitchell in every month of the year.

**4**

What African American educator would characterize conditions in antebellum North Carolina as "more lenient than those of any other Southern state. The result was that many free Negroes crossed into North Carolina and settled, undisturbed, in the northern and southern counties"?

**5**

How many deaths have been attributed to shark attacks in twentieth-century North Carolina: four, forty, or four hundred?

**6**

"Carolina" is a Latinized version of what name?

**7**

"The Putter Boy," a youngster in baggy pants and floppy hat, is the longtime symbol of what resort town?

**8**

What Edgecombe County town is the nation's oldest chartered by African Americans?

**9**

Among the artifacts on display at the museum at Fort Raleigh on Roanoke Island is a complete, furnished room from an English castle, circa 1600. How did it get there?

**10**

What president was once a member of the Rowan County bar?

**11**

What Guilford County native appeared on the cover of the first issue of *Time* magazine in 1923?

**12**

North Carolina's first visit from an occupied UFO was reported in 1952. Where did it take place?

**13**

What U.S. senator was born in North Wilkesboro?

**14**

The North Carolina chapter of the American Institute of Architects is headquartered in what unique Raleigh landmark?

## 15

Sugar Ray Leonard, Charles Kuralt, and Whistler's mother were all born in what city?

## 16

William Jennings Bryan delivered the opening address there, F. Scott Fitzgerald wrote there, William Howard Taft recuperated there, Béla Bartók composed there, and Margaret Mitchell honeymooned there. Where and what is it?

## 17

In 1930 Currituck County philanthropist Joseph Knapp founded the More Game Birds in America Foundation. By what name is the organization known today?

## 18

In 1792 Joel Lane sold a thousand acres of his Wake County plantation for what purpose?

## 19

True or false: Murphy, in the state's western corner, is closer to St. Louis than to Raleigh.

## 20

Winston and Salem joined to become a single city in what year: 1873, 1893, or 1913?

## 21

The government said the purpose of Fontana Dam, opened in western North Carolina in 1945, was to provide electricity to make aluminum. In reality, however, who was its main beneficiary?

## 22

Which two governors have both a county and two towns named after them?

**23**

True or false: North Carolina's state tree is the dogwood.

**24**

How old was George Washington Vanderbilt in 1888, when he began purchasing the land that would become the Biltmore Estate: twenty-five, forty-five, or sixty-five?

**25**

In reality, the "U.S. Navy Supply Center" at Harvey Point on the Albemarle Sound is a key facility of what government organization?

**26**

What do the people for whom Iredell and Moore Counties were named have in common?

**27**

At seventeen stories, this courthouse has been the tallest in North Carolina since it opened in 1928. Where is it?

**28**

When John Lawson trekked through the Piedmont in 1701, he noted that the trees were so tall that his party "saw plenty" of these birds, "but pearch'd upon such lofty Oaks, that our Guns would not kill them, tho' we shot very often, and our Guns were very good." What were the birds?

**29**

In what North Carolina city was a UFO reported in 1897?

**30**

According to George Washington's diary of his 1791 tour of the South, what town welcomed him with "as good a salute as could be given by one piece of artillery"?

**31**

True or false: North Carolina has no remaining covered bridges.

**32**

When did the earliest recorded sightings of coyotes in North Carolina occur: the 1730s, the 1830s, or the 1930s?

**33**

What U.S. president reported seeing the legendary Maco Light?

**34**

What 1961 incident was later documented as the closest the nation has come to suffering an atomic weapons disaster?

**35**

North Carolina's highest and lowest confirmed modern-day temperatures are 110°F and −34°F. Where were they recorded?

**36**

In what order did major hurricanes Donna, Fran, and Hazel hit the North Carolina coast?

**37**

Lord Cornwallis stayed there in 1781, Aaron Burr in 1796, and Gen. William T. Sherman in 1865. What's the name of this Hillsborough landmark?

**38**

Since succumbing to a storm off Cape Hatteras in 1862, the USS *Monitor* has rested at the bottom of the ocean at what depth: 230 feet, 2,300 feet, or 23,000 feet?

**39**

With which of these world cities is Charlotte on the same latitude: Tokyo, London, Paris, or Rome?

**40**

What is North Carolina's "fall line"?

**41**

The first SOS, from a disabled steamer, was received by a wireless operator on Cape Hatteras. Was it sent in 1909, 1919, or 1929?

**42**

What city is eternally split over whether to refer to its central business district as "uptown" or "downtown"?

**43**

In 1948 North Carolina suffered the nation's worst epidemic of what disease?

**44**

What unexplained topographical phenomenon has been described from the air as resembling a series of gigantic thumbprints?

**45**

True or false: Within ten miles of Grandfather Mountain exist twice as many varieties of plant life as in all of Europe.

**46**

What town has been described as "the Southern Part of Heaven"?

**47**

Brook trout, brown trout, and rainbow trout
are all found in the North Carolina mountains,
but only one is native. Which one?

**48**

What mountain town attracted so many Floridi-
ans during the 1920s that it became known as
"Little Miami"?

**49**

Who described the Venus's-flytrap, a carnivo-
rous plant that grows naturally only within a
seventy-five-mile radius of Wilmington, as "the
most wonderful little plant in the world"?

**50**

In 1524 Giovanni da Verrazano, sailing for the
French government, looked across the Outer
Banks and saw the Pamlico Sound. But what
did he think he was seeing?

**51**

Which state has more shoreline on the Atlantic
Ocean: North Carolina or Florida?

**52**

True or false: Canton is named for Canton,
Ohio.

**53**

According to the 1990 census, the population
of what North Carolina county ranks first
in percentage of southern-born and last in
percentage of foreign-born?

**54**

What county's population has the highest
percentage of "Yankees"?

## 55

Which of these is *not* a community in North Carolina: Lizard Lick, Loafers Glory, Possumtrot, Pumpkin Center, Social Circle?

## 56

What lake once ranked among the world's largest farms?

## 57

Match each town with its former name:

| Beaufort | Burnt Chimney |
| Cary | Fishtown |
| Dunn | Page's Siding |
| Forest City | Tearshirt |

## 58

A near-shipwreck in 1585 resulted in the first known reference to what point on the North Carolina coast?

## 59

In an effort to make Carolina less intimidating to potential colonists, promoters tried to give Cape Fear a new name. What was it?

## 60

True or false: A 1997 survey of Jews in Mecklenburg County showed that fewer had been born there than in New York City.

## 61

Beaufort on the North Carolina coast and Beaufort on the South Carolina coast share a spelling but not a pronunciation. How do they differ?

## 62

True or false: Though each had a North Carolina city named in his honor, Sir Walter Raleigh never saw Raleigh, George Washington never saw Washington, and the Marquis de Lafayette never saw Fayetteville.

**63**

Which is farthest south: Greenville, S.C.; Columbia, S.C.; or Wilmington, N.C.?

**64**

What Spanish explorer trekked across North Carolina in 1540 in his futile search for El Dorado: Hernando de Soto, Hernando Cortés, or Ponce de Leon?

**65**

Is the geographic center of North Carolina closest to Sanford, Siler City, or Southern Pines?

**66**

Which of these labels was applied to early North Carolina: the Turpentine State, the Old North State, the Rip Van Winkle State, or the Ireland of America?

**67**

In addition to South Carolina, Tennessee, and Virginia, what other state shares a border with North Carolina?

**68**

What was North Carolina's largest city in 1790? in 1890? in 1990?

**69**

How do North Carolina, North Dakota, and North Korea rank in area?

**70**

True or false: North Carolina has more state-maintained roads than any other state.

**71**

In what year did the town of Hillsboro return to its original, colonial spelling of "Hillsborough": 1925, 1945, or 1965?

**72**

What county is more than two-thirds water?

**73**

What was the fate of the onetime Rockingham County towns of Leaksville, Draper, and Spray?

**74**

What name was given to the route taken by Scots-Irish settlers from Pennsylvania and Maryland as they began populating the Carolina backcountry in the 1740s?

**75**

True or false: The 1980 census was the first since Reconstruction to report more people moving into North Carolina than moving out.

**76**

In the 1990s, what state bumped North Carolina from its No. 10 ranking in population?

**77**

"Hoi toid" (high tide) is an example of what dialect?

**78**

The dialect in what other part of the state most resembles the Outer Banks brogue?

**79**

What is the highest incorporated town east of the Mississippi River?

**80**

Which city is wetter, Seattle or Charlotte?

**81**

What do the cities of Minneapolis, Baltimore, Cleveland, Denver, Nashville, Washington, Honolulu, and Dallas have in common?

**82**

The official flag of what North Carolina city features a snarling bear?

**83**

How many lighthouses stand along the North Carolina coast?

**84**

Who was the previous owner of Wildacres, the property near Mount Mitchell where Charlotte industrialist I. D. Blumenthal founded a human relations center?

**85**

What do Charlotteans mean when they refer to the "'Ch'-factor"?

**86**

Geologists say that before millions of years of erosion, this mountain range extending across Montgomery, Randolph, and Stanly Counties stood higher than the Rockies. What is it?

**87**

In the traditional lexicon of the Outer Banks, what is a "dingbatter"?

## 88

What was North Carolina's first incorporated town?

## 89

Of North Carolina's one hundred counties, how many are named for women?

## 90

When it opened in 1965, this twenty-seven-story skyscraper was the South's tallest. What was it?

## 91

What modern-day North Carolina city was previously known as New Liverpool, Newton, and New Town?

## 92

What three North Carolina counties are named for presidents?

## 93

Which is farthest west: Charlotte, Miami, or Pittsburgh?

## 94

What mountain range lies within a single North Carolina county?

## 95

Which is taller, the Statue of Liberty (from toe to torch) or the Cape Hatteras Lighthouse?

## 96

The art deco Reynolds Building in Winston-Salem served as a model for what New York landmark?

# ANSWERS

**1**

The Pacific Ocean. The plane would be off the coast of Colombia.

**2**

Fifteen miles per hour. In town, speed limits were as low as six miles per hour.

**3**

True.

**4**

Booker T. Washington. In 1860, North Carolina was home to more than 30,000 free blacks, out of a total black population of 361,522.

**5**

Four, the most recent of which occurred off Atlantic Beach in 1957. (Shark attacks worldwide rarely occur until water temperatures reach 85°F, several degrees above North Carolina's maximum.)

**6**

Charles. When King Charles II granted a charter to the region between Virginia and Florida in 1663, he named the territory for himself.

**7**

Pinehurst, which bills itself as the Golf Capital of the World.

**8**

Princeville, settled by former slaves at the end of the Civil War.

**9**

William Randolph Hearst, a collector of Old World treasures, bought the room and had it dismantled and shipped to America. It never reached San Simeon, Hearst's California castle, and eventually fell into the hands of the National Park Service, which uncrated and displayed it at Fort Raleigh.

**10**

Andrew Jackson, who was admitted at age twenty and practiced law in Salisbury for several years before moving to Tennessee.

**11**

The autocratic Speaker of the House of Representatives, "Uncle Joe" Cannon of Illinois. The Cannon family moved to Illinois when he was a young man.

**12**

Lumberton. A saucer-shaped craft about ten feet in diameter supposedly struck the chimney of the home of businessman James Allen, then landed in his yard. The three-foot-tall occupant emerged, failed to respond to Allen's inquiries, and returned to the craft, which departed with an intense whistling sound.

**13**

Robert Byrd, the West Virginia Democrat.

**14**

The city's former water tower, built of granite and brick in 1887.

**15**

Wilmington.

**16**

The Grove Park Inn in Asheville, billed as "the finest resort hotel in the world" when it opened in 1913.

**17**

Ducks Unlimited, which now has 553,000 members.

**18**

To provide a site for North Carolina's permanent capital, Raleigh.

**19**

True.

**20**

1913.

**21**

The Manhattan Project at Oak Ridge, Tennessee. The super-secret project produced highly enriched uranium for the atomic bomb that exploded over Hiroshima eight months after the dam opened.

**22**

Zebulon Baird Vance gave his name to the county of Vance and the towns of Zebulon and Vanceboro, while Ashe County, Asheville, and Asheboro are all named for Samuel Ashe.

**23**

False. The state tree is the pine (the dogwood is the state flower).

**24**

He was twenty-five, youngest of eight children of railroad tycoon William Henry Vanderbilt, reputedly the world's richest man.

**25**

The CIA, which has trained thousands of U.S. and foreign officers there since 1961.

**26**

James Iredell of Edenton and Alfred Moore of New Hanover County are the only two North Carolinians ever to serve on the U.S. Supreme Court.

**27**

Asheville, Buncombe County.

**28**

"Turkies," as he spelled it in his journal.

**29**

Wilmington. According to the *Wilmington Messenger*, which headlined its account, "Was It an Air Ship?," hundreds of citizens spotted the "remarkable . . . brilliantly lighted" object as it floated above the city, creating "a sensation among all classes of people."

**30**

Tarboro.

**31**

False. It has two: The Pisgah Bridge in Randolph County and the Bunker Hill Bridge in Catawba County.

**32**

The 1930s. Since then, the eastward-migrating coyote has taken advantage of the decline of the wolf and driven the red fox from its former territory.

**33**

Grover Cleveland, when his train stopped one night in 1889 to take on wood and water at Maco, near Wilmington. Twenty-two years earlier, flagman Joe Baldwin had been decapitated while trying to wave off an oncoming locomotive. Baldwin's ghost supposedly continues to search for his head, carrying a lantern that can be seen as a bobbing glow in the distance.

**34**

When a B-52 bomber from Seymour Johnson Air Force Base crashed near Goldsboro, one of its 24-megaton atomic bombs snagged in a tree and was only a final safety catch away from detonation. Eastern North Carolina would have experienced an explosion 1,800 times more powerful than the one that leveled Hiroshima.

**35**

The highest was in Fayetteville in August 1983, the lowest at Mount Mitchell in January 1985.

**36**

Hazel, 1954; Donna, 1960; Fran, 1996.

**37**

The Colonial Inn, built in 1759 and now billed as the nation's oldest continuously operating inn.

**38**

Two hundred thirty feet.

**39**

Tokyo. The European cities are all farther
north.

**40**

The point where the rocky, rolling hills of
the Piedmont meet the flat, sandy soil of the
Coastal Plain. The fall line, an ancient coastline
marked by falls and rapids in the Roanoke, Tar,
Neuse and Cape Fear Rivers, runs just west of
modern-day Interstate 95.

**41**

1909.

**42**

Charlotte.

**43**

Polio. About 2,500 cases and 100 deaths were
reported that year. In 1959, North Carolina
became the first state to require children to be
inoculated with the new Salk vaccine.

**44**

The Carolina Bays. These shallow, oval impressions, rimmed with white sand, are all aligned
northwest to southeast along the Coastal Plain.
First reported in the late 1700s, they're not
bays at all, although some are filled with water.
Many are thickly overgrown with trees (including the bay trees for which they are named),
briers, and meat-eating plants. Most common
explanation: meteorites.

**45**

True.

**46**

Chapel Hill.

**47**

Brook trout. Brown trout were introduced from Europe, rainbow trout from the western United States.

**48**

Hendersonville.

**49**

Charles Darwin.

**50**

The Pacific Ocean.

**51**

North Carolina, with 3,375 miles to Florida's 3,331.

**52**

True. A foundry there produced the town's iron bridge, built across the Pigeon River in 1893.

**53**

Anson County, where 97.2 percent of residents were born in the South and .3 percent were born outside the United States.

**54**

Dare County, where 15.7 percent of residents were born in the Northeast.

**55**

Social Circle is in Georgia.

**56**

Lake Mattamuskeet in Hyde County. The shallow lake, eighteen miles long and six miles wide, was drained three times by ambitious promoters in the early decades of the 1900s. Its bottomland produced mammoth harvests of corn, rice, soybeans, and sweet potatoes, but operating problems finally won out. In 1934 the federal government bought the tract and created the Mattamuskeet Migratory Bird Refuge.

**57**

Beaufort, Fishtown; Cary, Page's Siding; Dunn, Tearshirt; Forest City, Burnt Chimney.

**58**

Cape Fear, or the "Cape of Feare."

**59**

Cape Fair. It didn't catch on.

**60**

True. Only 21 percent were born in Mecklenburg, compared with 24 percent born in New York state (almost all in New York City). An additional 14 percent were born elsewhere in the Northeast.

**61**

It's "BOH-fort" in North Carolina, "BYEW-fort" in South Carolina.

**62**

False. Lafayette visited Fayetteville in 1825.

**63**

Columbia. Greenville, S.C., is farthest north.

**64**

De Soto.

**65**

Sanford.

**66**

All of them.

**67**

Georgia, for about seventy-five miles.

**68**

Salisbury, 1790; Wilmington, 1890; Charlotte, 1990.

**69**

North Dakota, 70,702 square miles; North Carolina, 52,669 square miles; North Korea, 46,540 square miles.

**70**

False. It's runner-up to Texas.

**71**

1965.

**72**

Dare County has 388 acres of land, 858 acres of water.

**73**

In 1967 they merged to form a new town, Eden. (Before citizens decided that Spray was a more dignified name, that town was known as Splashy, after the water thrown up by the wheel at a local mill.)

**74**

The Great Wagon Road.

**75**

True.

**76**

Georgia.

**77**

The Outer Banks or Ocracoke brogue, described by some linguists as a remnant of Elizabethan or Shakespearean English.

**78**

The mountains, partly because the inhabitants share a common Scots-Irish ancestry, partly because the regions are similarly isolated.

**79**

Beech Mountain (altitude 5,506 feet).

**80**

Charlotte, with about forty-four inches of annual precipitation to Seattle's thirty-seven inches.

**81**

Each shares its name with a much smaller community in North Carolina.

**82**

New Bern, which took its name from Bern, Switzerland. *Bern* is Swiss for "bear."

**83**

Seven: Cape Lookout, Ocracoke, Cape Hatteras, Bodie Island, and Currituck Beach on the Outer Banks; Oak Island and Bald Head Island on the southern coast.

**84**

Thomas Dixon, author of *The Clansman*, the book that was made into *Birth of a Nation*. Dixon lost his second fortune when the crash of 1929 left him holding worthless investments on Wall Street, in Florida real estate, and at the 1,400-acre mountain tract he dreamed of turning into an elite resort and think tank.

Blumenthal bought it at auction in 1936 for $6,500.

**85**

The tendency of outsiders to confuse the city with Charleston, S.C., Charleston, W.Va., and Charlottesville, Va.

**86**

The Uwharries.

**87**

An outsider. Other examples: to be harassed is to be "mommucked"; to feel nauseated is to be "quamished"; an Ocracoke Islander is an "O'cocker."

**88**

Bath, laid out by John Lawson on the Pamlico River and incorporated in 1705.

**89**

Three: Dare County, named for Virginia Dare, first child of English parents born in the New World; Wake County, named for Margaret Wake, wife of colonial governor William Tryon; and Mecklenburg County, named for Princess Charlotte Sophia of Mecklenburg-Strelitz, wife of George III.

**90**

The Wachovia building in Winston-Salem. Today that distinction belongs to the sixty-story Bank of America headquarters in Charlotte.

**91**

Wilmington.

**92**

Washington, Madison, and Jackson. (Cleveland, Lincoln, Polk, and Wilson Counties are not.)

**93**

Charlotte.

**94**

The Sauratowns, which take up about 5 percent of Stokes County.

**95**

The lighthouse, at 208 feet to the Statue of Liberty's 151 feet. When its pedestal is included, the statue stands 305 feet.

**96**

The Empire State Building. New York architects Shreve and Lamb designed both the 102-story Empire State Building and, two years earlier, the 22-story Reynolds Building, headquarters for R. J. Reynolds. When the Reynolds Building celebrated its fiftieth anniversary in 1979, officials of the Empire State Building sent a card inscribed, "Happy Anniversary, Dad."

# WARS, ELECTIONS, AND OTHER DIFFERENCES OF OPINION

*You forget, sir, that you are a Yankee and that Plymouth is a Southern town. It is no business of yours if we choose to burn one of our own towns. A meddling Yankee troubles himself about everybody's matters except his own and repents of everybody's sins except his own. We are a different people. Should the Yankees burn a Union village in Connecticut or a codfish town in Massachusetts we would not meddle with them but rather bid them God speed in their work of purifying the atmosphere.*

*Your second act of forgetfulness consists in your not remembering that you are the most atrocious house-burner as yet unhung in the wide universe.*

*Confederate Maj. Gen. Daniel Harvey Hill, responding by letter to Union Maj. Gen. John Gray Foster, who had censured Hill for the burning of Plymouth during a battle in 1863*

*Your newspaper is a suck-egg mule.*

*Sen. Jesse Helms, confronting a reporter from the* Raleigh News and Observer *at a 1983 campaign breakfast*

# QUESTIONS

**1**

True or false: More than twenty-five times as many North Carolinians died in the Civil War as in the Vietnam War.

**2**

To what was Richard Petty referring when he said, "I mean, prestigious-wise, it's nothing like racing, you know what I mean?"?

**3**

In 1898 the nation's only daily newspaper for African Americans was the *Daily Record,* published in Wilmington. What happened to it?

**4**

The largest *Voice of America* relay station in the United States, built near Greenville in 1960, was situated to reach listeners in what city?

**5**

What animal attacked and fatally wounded a justice of the state supreme court in 1793?

**6**

Who attributed Hurricane Hugo to "the way people in Charlotte, North Carolina, have treated God's people"?

**7**

When did the last public hanging in North Carolina take place: 1870, 1890, or 1910?

**8**

What North Carolina gubernatorial candidate got a free plug in a 1960 installment of the comic strip *Pogo?*

**9**

In 1870 Hiram Revels, a Fayetteville native and onetime Lincolnton barbershop owner, was sworn in as U.S. senator from Mississippi – the first African American senator. Who was his predecessor?

**10**

During a 1925 debate, what Burke County legislator argued that a resolution discouraging the teaching of evolution did nothing more than "absolve monkeys from all responsibility for the human race"?

**11**

When four black freshmen from North Carolina A&T University asked to be served at the whites-only Woolworth lunch counter in downtown Greensboro in 1960, they not only set off a historic challenge to segregation across the South but also popularized a word describing their protest. What is it?

**12**

To what was Gov. Thomas Bickett referring when he claimed in a 1918 speech, "They will yield more solid comfort for the inner man than possum and potatoes, and more juicy sweetness than the apples for which our first ancestor threw Paradise away"?

## 13

In 1981, three days after shooting President Ronald Reagan, where was John Hinckley Jr. sent for psychiatric evaluation?

## 14

On April 2, 1968, Martin Luther King Jr. was assassinated after being called to Memphis to support striking sanitation workers. Where had he originally been scheduled to appear on that day?

## 15

What crucial role did North Carolina play in Ronald Reagan's political career?

## 16

What terse quotation marks the tombstone of William Lawrence Saunders, who was North Carolina's secretary of state at the time of his death in 1891?

## 17

What civil rights activist spent twenty-two days on an Orange County chain gang in 1947 for testing a state law requiring segregated seating on buses?

## 18

Who was the 1972 Democratic senatorial candidate whose lengthy Greek surname inspired his campaign staff to split it into two buttons?

## 19

When John Spencer Bassett, professor at Trinity College (later Duke University), wrote in 1903 about the person whom he considered "the greatest man, save General Lee, born in the South in a hundred years," he put his job at risk and precipitated a national free speech cause célèbre. Who was the subject of Bassett's praise?

## 20

What decorative object at the Hickory home of Congressman Cass Ballenger caused a racial dispute in 1994?

## 21

In the 1984 race for governor, Rufus Edmisten committed a major blunder when he grumbled that he couldn't choke down another "damnable" bite of what?

## 22

In 1819, after reading a latter-day copy of this document, John Adams sang its praises in a letter to Thomas Jefferson: "What a poor, ignorant, malicious, short-sighted, crapulous mass is Tom Paine's 'Common Sense,' in comparison. . . . The genuine sense of America at that moment was never expressed so well before, nor since." To what was Adams referring?

## 23

Jesse Helms teasingly sang "Dixie" to what fellow U.S. senator during a 1993 Capitol Hill elevator ride: Strom Thurmond, Edward Kennedy, or Carol Moseley-Braun?

## 24

What was "Scannergate"?

## 25

What is Swain County's "road to nowhere"?

**26**

The question "Where do you stand, Jim?" played a central role in what political campaign?

**27**

What president assured North Carolinians that the government's antismoking campaign was intended only "to make the smoking of tobacco even more safe than it is today"?

**28**

In the twentieth century, what two North Carolinians have won election to both the U.S. Senate and the governorship?

**29**

Overcoming intense resistance from tobacco interests, North Carolina first imposed a tax on cigarettes in what year: 1929, 1949, or 1969?

**30**

The notorious Andersonville prison camp was the Confederacy's largest. What was the second largest?

**31**

Which member of O. J. Simpson's legal Dream Team had previously represented Jim Bakker: Alan Dershowitz, Johnnie Cochran, or F. Lee Bailey?

**32**

What influential civil rights organization was founded at Shaw University in Raleigh?

**33**

Thanks to a persuasive 1973 floor speech by mountain legislator Herbert Hyde, North Carolina law still specifies two counties "where a man can go and ——— with impunity." What right was Hyde defending?

## 34

What future U.S. senator was almost killed in a 1984 plane crash?

## 35

The first North Carolina resident to appear on the cover of *Time* magazine was Henry L. Stevens Jr., a lawyer from Warsaw, in 1932. What had he done?

## 36

Junius Scales of Chapel Hill was the only American ever to spend time in prison for what offense?

## 37

Who attended the Edenton Tea Party?

## 38

True or false: Sam J. Ervin Jr. never lost an election.

## 39

What law enforcement official referred to Gaston B. Means, born in Cabarrus County and educated at the University of North Carolina at Chapel Hill, as "the worst crook I ever knew"?

## 40

What famous Civil War general was fatally shot by troops from the 18th North Carolina Regiment?

## 41

What controversial slogan was imprinted on North Carolina license plates in the mid-1970s?

## 42

In 1944 Rep. Carl Durham of North Carolina blocked circulation of a booklet aimed at troops overseas. Why?

## 43

True or false: The "King" in Seattle's Kingdome was originally William Rufus DeVane King, the Sampson County native elected vice president in 1852, though the arena was later "renamed" for Martin Luther King Jr.

## 44

Though he didn't have a speaking part, what future North Carolina political figure received hours of national television exposure during the Senate Watergate hearings?

## 45

What was the site of the bloodiest battle ever fought on North Carolina soil?

## 46

The Christopher Reynolds Foundation, established after the mountain-climbing death of the seventeen-year-old son of Z. Smith Reynolds and Libby Holman, financed what civil rights leader's momentous pilgrimage to India to learn the passive resistance strategies of Mahatma Gandhi?

## 47

Former N.C. congressman Earl Ruth's misadventures as governor of American Samoa were satirized in what comic strip?

## 48

True or false: Less than a year before Pearl Harbor, the N.C. legislature foreshadowed the

creation of the United Nations with a resolution stating: "There is no alternative to the
federation of all nations except endless war."

**49**

What was the site of the Civil War's largest
sea-land battle?

**50**

How many North Carolinians who died in the
Spanish-American War are *not* commemorated
with public monuments?

**51**

In what year did North Carolina elect its first
Republican governor and U.S. senator since the
turn of the century: 1952, 1962, or 1972?

**52**

In 1865, with the end of the Civil War in sight,
more than a thousand soldiers and several
cannon were involved in the five-hour battle of
Asheville. How many deaths were reported?

**53**

Tapes made by Winston-Salem screenwriter
Laura Hart McKinny undercut the credibility
of which key prosecution witness in the O. J.
Simpson murder trial?

**54**

According to the last census before the Civil
War, there were three hundred southerners
who owned at least three hundred slaves each.
How many of these large-scale slaveowners
were North Carolinians: four, forty, or one
hundred?

**55**

William "Manny" Tager, a Charlotte man imprisoned for the fatal 1994 shooting of an NBC stagehand in New York, was later linked to what other notorious incident?

**56**

True or false: A quarter-century after the battle of Bentonville, the losing Confederate general served as a pallbearer at the winning Union general's funeral.

**57**

What incident in Greensboro may have decided the 1960 presidential election?

**58**

In 1941 the Charlotte City Council changed the name of Lindbergh Drive to Avon Terrace. Why?

**59**

True or false: The first Freedom Riders, headed from Washington to Jackson, Miss., to challenge the South's segregrated bus facilities, made it through North Carolina without incident.

**60**

Where did Henry Clay write the memorable words, "I had rather be right than be president"?

**61**

Mel Watt and Eva Clayton, both elected in 1992, were the state's first African American members of Congress since what year: 1901, 1921, or 1941?

## 62

In 1919 Margaret Sanger gave the South's first public lecture on birth control. Was it in Chapel Hill, Charlotte, or Elizabeth City?

## 63

Which 2000 presidential contender graduated from Duke? Which one accepted a scholarship from Duke but backed out at the last moment?

# ANSWERS

**1**

True. The Civil War claimed 40,275 soldiers from North Carolina; the Vietnam War, 1,596.

**2**

The office of N.C. secretary of state, for which he was an unsuccessful candidate in 1996.

**3**

Vigilantes, part of a campaign to reestablish white supremacy in the state, destroyed the press and burned down the building. Eleven African Americans died in the riot that followed, and whites took over the city government. It would be 1927 before Wilmington had another black newspaper.

**4**

Moscow.

**5**

A turkey. Samuel Spencer was sitting on the porch of his home near Wadesboro when he became sleepy and began to nod off; his bobbing red cap apparently provoked a nearby turkey gobbler to attack. The fifty-nine-year-old judge was thrown from his chair and suffered numerous scratches, which became infected, with fatal results.

**6**

Tammy Faye Bakker, whose husband was on trial in a Charlotte courtroom when the hurricane hit in 1989. Televangelist Jim Bakker was found guilty of defrauding contributors to his PTL ministry and served five years in prison.

**7**

1910. In Elizabethtown, Henry Spivey was executed for the murder of his father-in-law.

**8**

Terry Sanford, whose campaign aide Roy Wilder persuaded cartoonist pal Walt Kelly to label Pogo's flat-bottomed swamp boat "Ol' Terry Sanford N.C."

**9**

Jefferson Davis, who had vacated the seat to become president of the Confederacy.

**10**

Future U.S. senator Sam J. Ervin Jr.

**11**

"Sit-in."

**12**

Liberty Bonds, which helped finance World War I.

**13**

The Federal Correctional Facility in Butner. Jim Bakker, the televangelist, and Jeffrey MacDonald, the former army physician convicted in 1979 of murdering his wife and daughters at Fort Bragg, were also held there.

**14**

In North Carolina, to campaign for gubernatorial candidate Reginald Hawkins, a Charlotte dentist. The telegram Hawkins received from the Southern Christian Leadership Conference in Atlanta said, "We will be in touch with you in the next two weeks regarding the new tour schedule."

**15**

In 1976 North Carolina Republicans, urged on by Sen. Jesse Helms, resuscitated Reagan's failing presidential campaign. After five defeats, Reagan scored his first primary victory over President Gerald Ford in North Carolina. Although he failed to win the nomination that year, his late-blooming primary victories established him as the GOP front runner in 1980.

**16**

"I decline to answer," his response to a Congressional committee investigating the Ku Klux Klan. Saunders, who had been severely wounded during the Civil War, was considered the Klan's chief strategist in the state.

**17**

Bayard Rustin, then a little-known, thirty-five-year-old Quaker from New York. Rustin's Journey of Reconciliation was essentially the first Freedom Ride. Later, as a key aide to Martin Luther King Jr., he would help organize the 1955 Montgomery bus boycott and the 1963 March on Washington for Jobs and Freedom, at which King gave his "I Have a Dream" speech.

## 18

Nick Galifianakis (GALIFI on one button, ANAKIS on the other). A Durham lawyer and former three-term U.S. congressman, Galifianakis lost to Raleigh TV editorialist Jesse Helms.

## 19

Booker T. Washington. Trinity trustees ultimately voted to reject Bassett's resignation, though not before Raleigh newspaper editor Josephus Daniels had repeatedly printed the professor's name as "bASSett."

## 20

A lawn jockey. The local NAACP chapter criticized it as "a reminder of the cotton-field days, the days when we were called 'boy.'" Ballenger said the cast-iron statue was a family heirloom nicknamed Rochester, after the black valet on the old *Jack Benny Show*, and refused to remove it.

## 21

Barbecue. Edmisten apologized at length but lost anyway.

## 22

The Mecklenburg Declaration of Independence, supposedly drawn up on May 20, 1775, more than a year before Jefferson's own Declaration of Independence, but destroyed in a fire in 1800. Jefferson scoffed that the Meck Dec was "spurious." Most historians since have agreed.

## 23

Moseley-Braun. Two weeks earlier, the black Democrat from Illinois had thwarted Helms's effort to renew a patent for a United Daughters of the Confederacy insignia that depicted a Confederate flag.

**24**

A 1992 campaign scandal. One of Gov. Jim Hunt's supporters and two of his former law partners were each sentenced to six months on probation for eavesdropping on cellular phone calls involving Jim Gardner, Hunt's Republican challenger.

**25**

A road promised by the federal government in 1943 but still unbuilt today. At the height of World War II, the government took land from Swain County for a 10,000-acre lake. (Today Fontana Dam, the highest in the eastern United States, produces electricity for the Tennessee Valley Authority.) Federal officials agreed in writing to provide the ousted residents access to family cemeteries, but the planned thirty-four-mile road was never finished, and later the area was incorporated, over intense local objections, into Great Smoky Mountains National Park.

**26**

Sen. Jesse Helms used the line in TV commercials that painted his 1984 Democratic challenger, Gov. Jim Hunt, as wishy-washy and calculatingly political. Hunt lost the Senate race, though he would later win third and fourth terms as governor. Together Helms and Hunt spent $26 million on their campaigns, more than any other two senatorial candidates in U.S. history.

**27**

Jimmy Carter, in 1978.

**28**

Clyde Hoey, elected governor in 1936 and senator in 1944 and 1950; Terry Sanford, elected
governor in 1960 and senator in 1986.

**29**

1969.

**30**

Salisbury Prison, built to hold 2,500 but eventually housing a peak of 8,740 men. More than
4,000 died there.

**31**

Dershowitz, who successfully appealed for a re-
duction in Bakker's forty-five-year sentence for
fraud. The sentence was cut first to eighteen
years, then eight, and Bakker actually served
only five years.

**32**

The Student Nonviolent Coordinating Committee (SNCC, pronounced "Snick").

**33**

The right to "cuss." For years, cursing in public
had been legal in Swain and Pitt Counties.
When a bill came up to end Pitt's exemption,
Hyde opposed it in a speech so colorful it was
made into a record.

**34**

Lauch Faircloth, who was campaigning for
governor when the small plane he was aboard
crashed in the shallows of a McDowell County
lake. Faircloth couldn't swim but managed
to escape from the partly submerged plane,

through burning gasoline, just before the main
fuel tank exploded.

**35**

As national commander of the American
Legion, Stevens opposed granting a cash bonus
to World War I veterans, an issue that culmi-
nated in the controversial "Bonus Army" march
on Washington.

**36**

Being a communist. At a 1954 trial in Greensboro, Scales, head of the Communist Party in
the Carolinas, was convicted of membership in
an organization advocating violent overthrow
of the government. Scales began serving a six-
year sentence in 1961; the next year President
Kennedy freed him by commuting his sentence
to parole on his own recognizance.

**37**

Fifty-one self-described "patriotic ladies," who
in 1774 met and resolved in writing to boycott
East Indian tea as long as it was taxed by the
British – one of the first organized political
actions by American women.

**38**

False. In 1926, making his first race for public
office, the thirty-year-old Ervin was defeated
for district solicitor.

**39**

J. Edgar Hoover, director of the FBI. Among
Means's career highlights: spying for Germany
against the British in the early days of World
War I; writing a book falsely alleging that President Harding's death had been murder; bilking
a wealthy Washington woman by claiming to

have made ransom arrangements with the kidnappers of the Lindbergh baby.

**40**

Thomas J. "Stonewall" Jackson, the Confederacy's master tactician. Jackson's men mistook him for the enemy while he was scouting ahead of the line at nightfall near Chancellorsville.

**41**

"First in Freedom." Intended as a tribute to the state's early role in the American Revolution, the slogan became a civil liberties issue when police arrested several motorists who had taped over it to protest capital punishment and racial inequality. The U.S. Supreme Court came down on the side of free speech, and the state abandoned the slogan when its supply of plates manufactured in Raleigh's Central Prison was exhausted.

**42**

He found blasphemous a drawing that depicted Adam and Eve with navels. By the congressman's reasoning, human beings made by God would have had no evidence of an umbilical cord.

**43**

Strange but true. In 1986 the King County Council voted to rename the county (and therefore the stadium) for the civil rights leader. Noted the council member who proposed the change: "We won't have to reprint stationery or change road signs or anything like that."

**44**

Rufus Edmisten, who sat directly behind his boss, committee chairman Sam Ervin. Edmisten later won election as attorney general and secretary of state.

**45**

Bentonville, in 1865. Gen. Joseph Johnston managed to surprise Sherman's larger force, but Union reinforcements arrived and turned the battle. Confederate losses totaled 2,600; Union losses, 1,600.

**46**

Dr. Martin Luther King Jr.

**47**

*Doonesbury,* in which Garry Trudeau bestowed the governorship on his character Uncle Duke.

**48**

True. The resolution remained on the books until 1995, when opponents successfully argued that it advocated "world government."

**49**

Fort Fisher. Determined to break at last what Robert E. Lee considered the lifeline of the Confederacy, fifty-eight Union warships in the Cape Fear River bombarded the fort for three days before sending ashore 5,300 troops, who overwhelmed the fort's 1,900 defenders in hand-to-hand combat. Union casualties exceeded 1,300; Confederate casualties, 500.

**50**

None. Ensign Worth Bagley is honored with a statue in Raleigh, army lieutenant William Shipp with an obelisk in Charlotte.

**51**

1972, when Governor Jim Holshouser and Senator Jesse Helms were both elected.

**52**

None.

**53**

Mark Fuhrman, Los Angeles police detective.

**54**

Four.

**55**

The 1986 mugging of CBS newsman Dan Rather. Rather told police he had been attacked on Park Avenue by a man who repeatly shouted, "What's the frequency, Kenneth?" The episode became part of modern-day folklore, making Rather the butt of jokes and inspiring the song "What's the Frequency, Kenneth?" by R.E.M. In 1997 a forensic psychiatrist named Tager as the likely mugger, and Rather identified him from a photograph. Because the statute of limitations had expired, no charges were filed.

**56**

True. Out of respect to William Tecumseh Sherman, Joseph Johnston went hatless at the chilly graveside, catching a cold that developed into a fatal infection.

**57**

Vice President Richard Nixon, in Greensboro for a campaign rally, banged his left kneecap on a car door. The injury became infected, causing him to be hospitalized and thereby miss two weeks of campaigning. He was still haggard and off-form when he arrived for his crucial first TV debate with Senator John F. Kennedy. As he got out of his car at the studio, Nixon again struck his knee on the door.

**58**

To dishonor Charles Lindbergh, for whom the street was originally named, for his opposition to U.S. involvement in the war against Germany.

**59**

False. They incurred their first arrest during an overnight stop in Charlotte. A black Freedom Rider was jailed for trespassing after being denied a shoeshine in the bus station's whites-only barbershop.

**60**

In Raleigh, where Clay was visiting when he composed a letter opposing the annexation of Mexico – an unpopular stand that did indeed scuttle his presidential hopes.

**61**

1901, when former slave George Henry White of Tarboro resigned his seat after the General Assembly disenfranchised African Americans.

**62**

Elizabeth City. Sanger, invited to speak by maverick newspaper editor W. O. Saunders, recalled later, "Never have I met with more sympathy, more serious attention, more complete understanding than in . . . this Southern mill town."

Elizabeth Dole graduated with Duke's Class of 1958. Bill Bradley (Princeton, 1965) accepted a basketball scholarship to Duke, then took a student tour of Europe and fell in love with Oxford. On returning, he learned that Princeton had produced more Rhodes Scholars than any other college. Goodbye, Duke. "In retrospect," Bradley wrote later, "that decision was the turning point of my life." He became an All-America basketball player at Princeton, a Rhodes Scholar, and an NBA star before taking up politics.

# ARTS AND LETTERS

*A lattice fence has been placed around the*
*commons outhouses and adds greatly to the*
*appearance of the place.*

The Tar Heel *newspaper, praising*
*improvements to the University of*
*North Carolina campus in 1887*


*What a surprise to enter a peacefully homo-*
*geneous community where money is never*
*mentioned, where no racial tension exists either*
*on or under any surface; & where instead of col-*
*liding with indoctrinated automata, one meets*
*courteous individuals! For the first time I realize*
*what "America" might have been.*

*Poet e. e. cummings, just back from a*
*1958 series of readings at North Carolina*
*colleges, sharing his impressions in a*
*letter to his sister*

# QUESTIONS

**1**

What famous book of poetry describes "the sounds and inlets of North Carolina's coast, the shad-fishery and the herring-fishery, the large sweep-seines, the windlasses on shore work'd by horses, the clearing, curing, and packing-houses"?

**2**

A 1965 *Life* magazine profile of Andrew Wyeth inspired what Lexington businessman to heed a long-dormant desire to become an artist?

**3**

In the 1920s Gutzon Borglum took time out from a major project in order to sculpt a monument at Gettysburg honoring North Carolina's Civil War dead. What was the work he interrupted?

**4**

Match the honorary graduate with the college:

| | |
|---|---|
| Ned Jarrett, NASCAR driver | Duke University |
| Ann Landers, columnist | Lenoir-Rhyne College |
| Johnny Cash, musician | UNC-Pembroke |
| Bill Cosby, actor | Gardner-Webb University |

**5**

True or false: Though now often associated with North Carolina, the term "Tobacco Road" was first used in reference to Georgia.

**6**

What are the chances that a Duke University undergraduate is a North Carolinian: one in two, one in four, or one in eight?

**7**

What Wake County town is named for the writer, physician, and philosopher who named the *Atlantic Monthly?*

**8**

Thomas Sully's *Washington at the Passage of the Delaware,* commissioned by the N.C. legislature in 1814, never hung in the statehouse as intended. Why?

**9**

Former governor Charles Brantley Aycock, whose administration pushed North Carolina schools decades ahead, dropped dead of a heart attack during a speech in Birmingham, Alabama, in 1912. What was his last word?

**10**

Florence King spent two years in Raleigh before writing *Southern Ladies and Gentlemen,* her 1975 acerbic guide to "Poor Things, Dear Old Things, and Good Ole Boys." What was her job?

**11**

What do the Dalai Lama, Henry Kissinger, Clarence Thomas, and Madeleine Albright have in common?

**12**

How many words did editor Maxwell Perkins trim from Thomas Wolfe's *Look Homeward, Angel:* 900, 9,000, or 90,000?

**13**

What future political figure spent much of his childhood on the campus of Charlotte's Biddle University, later Johnson C. Smith University, where his grandfather was president?

**14**

What president of the Duke University student bar association was recognized on the banquet program with a caricature captioned "Our New Prexy 'Nose' All"?

**15**

To what were the following nicknames once attached: Princeton of the South, Paris of the South, Chicago of the South, and Mouth of the South?

**16**

True or false: The University of Georgia was the first state university to be chartered, in 1785, but the University of North Carolina was the first to admit students, in 1795.

**17**

"At the first gesture of morning, flies began stirring." In what novel is this the opening sentence?

**18**

What city's board of aldermen voted in 1889 to trim the budget by eliminating "eighth-grade education in the graded schools at public expense"?

## 19

What celebrated writer now living in North Carolina was born Marguerite Johnson?

## 20

Match the modern-day college with its predecessor:

| | |
|---|---|
| Guilford College | Woman's College |
| N.C. State University | N.C. College for Negroes |
| N.C. Central University | New Garden Boarding School |
| UNC-Greensboro | N.C. College of Agricultural and Mechanic Arts |

## 21

What university, founded as Croatan Normal School, was for many years attended only by American Indians?

## 22

Hearing Eudora Welty read her short story "Why I Live at the P.O." on public television provoked what Campbell College professor to start writing fiction?

## 23

About his time at what college did novelist William Styron recall, "My innate sinfulness was in constant conflict with the prevailing official piety"?

## 24

Alex Haley conceived *Roots* while researching his slave ancestors in what county?

**25**

Vollis Simpson of Lucama, Clyde Jones of Bynum, and James Harold Jennings of Pinnacle have attracted national recognition in what field?

**26**

What syndicated comic strip based its protagonist on a University of North Carolina journalism professor?

**27**

What was North Carolina's last male-only college?

**28**

In the space of one year, this folksy essayist had two No. 1 *New York Times* bestsellers. His first book was still on the list in 1959 when the second one debuted – the first time that had ever happened. Who was he?

**29**

In 1795 Hinton James of Wilmington became the first student to enroll at the University of North Carolina. How many faculty members were there?

**30**

Her 1943 first novel was the first book by a woman to spend more than a year on the *New York Times* bestseller list. Who was she?

**31**

Laurinburg Institute, one of the nation's few remaining African American prep schools, grew out of a request for help to what well-known educator?

## 32

*Something of Value,* his lurid 1955 novel about
a Mau Mau uprising, reached No. 1 on the
bestseller list, became a movie starring Rock
Hudson and Sidney Poitier, and provoked *New
York Times* critic Orville Prescott to declare it
the most loathsome book he had read in nearly
twenty-five years of reviewing. Who was the
author?

## 33

Match the graduate with his or her historically
black college:

| | |
|---|---|
| Sarah and A. Elizabeth Delany | St. Augustine's |
| Earl "The Pearl" Monroe | N.C. A&T |
| Dan Blue | Winston-Salem State |
| Ron McNair | N.C. Central |

## 34

The protagonist of what 1980 novel lived in Linwood, "the most Christian town . . . in the most
Christian state in the South, North Carolina"?

## 35

What North Carolina town is named after an
Italian sculptor?

## 36

In his 1989 book *A Turn in the South,* V. S.
Naipaul is struck by the similarity between the
swept-dirt front yards of Wilson County and
those in his native land. What country is that?

**37**

What art form that predates Michelangelo does
North Carolina enjoy in greater abundance
than any other state?

**38**

Touted as the next *Bridges of Madison
County,* Nicholas Sparks's 1996 first novel did
indeed become a long-lived bestseller. In what
North Carolina city where Sparks had once
lived did *The Notebook* take place?

**39**

North Carolina's two classic equestrian statues
are in Greensboro and Winston-Salem. Whom
do they commemorate?

**40**

At a 1963 meeting of the Southern Historical
Association in Asheville, University of Mississippi professor James Silver gave the first
public preview of what controversial book
about segregation?

**41**

*Laughing All the Way* was the title of what
Raleigh native's 1973 memoir of her years as
Washington's most publicized hostess and
social commentator?

**42**

What North Carolinian did colleague Calvin
Trillin cite as "the *New Yorker* reporter who
set the standard"?

**43**

From scribbled notes on an early manuscript,
Wilmington document examiner Maureen

Casey Owens confirmed the identity of the author of what political roman à clef?

**44**

After a visit in 1905, what renowned writer described Biltmore House as "utterly unaddressed to any possible arrangement of life . . . a gorgeous practical joke"?

**45**

Match the North Carolina writer with his or her novel:

| | |
|---|---|
| Lee Smith | *Ellen Foster* |
| Allen Gurganus | *A Short History of a Small Place* |
| Gail Godwin | *Oldest Living Confederate Widow Tells All* |
| T. R. Pearson | *Fair and Tender Ladies* |
| Kaye Gibbons | *Father Melancholy's Daughter* |

**46**

The memorable description of North Carolina as "a valley of humility between two mountains of conceit" originated in what year: 1800, 1850, or 1900?

**47**

Who is the youngest author ever to have a No. 1 nonfiction book on the *New York Times* bestseller list?

**48**

How many works by Rembrandt are owned by the North Carolina Museum of Art?

**49**

What UNC–Chapel Hill sociologist has delineated the South by such techniques as counting "Dixie" listings in local telephone directories?

**50**

In 1990 a whimsical "playing field" of seven spherically pruned holly bushes was installed on a sloping median in front of the Charlotte Coliseum. For what previous public art work was architect Maya Lin best known?

**51**

Patricia Cornwell is best known for her Kay Scarpetta crime novels, but her first book was a biography. Who was the subject of 1983's *A Time for Remembering?*

**52**

One of this abstract expressionist's best-known works was painted in the North Carolina mountains during the summer of 1948, when he joined the faculty of Black Mountain College. The painting's title was *Asheville*. Who was the painter?

**53**

Fred Chappell, a professor at UNC-Greensboro, and Sam Ragan, a newspaperman from Southern Pines who died in 1996, are the only two writers ever to hold this position. What is it?

**54**

In his comprehensive *The Architecture of the United States*, G. E. Kidder Smith calls what North Carolina structure "the world's most superb example of three-dimensional, functional graphics"?

**55**

What two controversial literary figures are buried a few feet from each other in Shelby?

**56**

The "thrust lines" of what Raleigh landmark have been compared to those of Mies van der Rohe's famed Barcelona chair?

**57**

In 1927 a friend in Paris wrote to thank Etta Cone, a member of the Greensboro textile family, for a shipment of apples from the Cone estate at Blowing Rock. They were "better than ever and larger and rosier and even more enjoyed," she said. Who was the correspondent?

**58**

What 1947 nonfiction bestseller includes the line, "The first thing I saw in North Carolina was a sign outside a group of bungalows, 'Motor Court Morally Pure' "?

**59**

Ray Hicks of Beech Mountain is one of the nation's most honored folk artists. What is his specialty?

**60**

"It came to me that I had been generally re-tracing the migration of my white-blooded clan from North Carolina to Missouri, the clan of Lancashiremen who settled in the Piedmont in the eighteenth century. As a boy, again and again, I had looked at a blurred, sepia photograph of a leaning tombstone deep in the Carolina hills. I had vowed to find the old immigrant miller's grave one day." From what popular 1982 book does this passage come?

**61**

Lovesick, this twenty-year-old aspiring poet took a train and steamer south from New England, then walked ten miles into the Great Dismal Swamp. His halfhearted idea of suicide was quickly forgotten, however, when he fell in with a party of drunken duck hunters from Elizabeth City. Who was he?

**62**

What Durham native is the author of *The Provincials: A Personal History of Jews in the South* and *The Lonely Days Were Sundays: Reflections of a Jewish Southerner?*

**63**

What two prominent literary figures are buried in Riverside Cemetery in Asheville?

**64**

What antebellum southern traveler wrote this in his diary: "Country about Raleigh is little cultivated. It is a mystery how inhabitants can obtain sufficient supplies from it to exist"?

**65**

Mitford is the fictional version of what North Carolina mountain town?

**66**

Gov. Terry Sanford envisioned a conservatory to rival the best in the Northeast; legislative critics envisioned a "toe-dancin' school." What was it?

**67**

What Duke University student did Reynolds Price recognize for writing fiction "as if a kind of perfect pitch had been inserted into her head by God"?

**68**

Why was his family less than enthusiastic about the eight-foot-tall bronze statue of Martin Luther King Jr. unveiled in Charlotte's Marshall Park in 1980?

**69**

What North Carolina college has the largest enrollment?

**70**

In *State v. Mann* in 1830, the North Carolina Supreme Court declined to address the institution of slavery. The case later served as background for what 1852 novel that energized and broadened the abolitionist movement?

**71**

In 1849 James K. Polk became the first president to have his picture taken in the White House. Who was the photographer?

**72**

What North Carolina writer was stunned to hear President Clinton repeat from memory the 189-word opening line of his 1962 first novel?

**73**

"Gaudy gullet of hell" was author Tom Wolfe's description of what North Carolina street?

**74**

What university was long known as
"Eecy-teecy"?

**75**

What writer never set foot in North Carolina
but used an 1874 series of earthquakes in
Rutherford County as inspiration for a novel?

**76**

Political figures Woodrow Wilson, Dean Rusk,
and Vince Foster were all alumni of what
college?

**77**

Among educational institutions for women in
the United States, what is the distinction of
Salem Academy and College in Winston-Salem?

**78**

What future mainstay of the Beat Generation
wrote a novel at his sister's kitchen table in
Rocky Mount in 1956?

**79**

What writer has characterized North Carolina
as "the bizarre murder center of the Earth"?

**80**

Which of these three celebrated UNC–Chapel
Hill alumni did *not* serve as editor of the *Daily
Tar Heel:* Thomas Wolfe, Charles Kuralt, or
Lawrence Ferlinghetti?

**81**

Visiting Charlotte's glitzy downtown, what
novelist marveled, "It makes you wonder who
won the War between the States"?

# ANSWERS

**1**

*Leaves of Grass,* by Walt Whitman, who never visited the state.

**2**

Bob Timberlake.

**3**

Mount Rushmore.

**4**

Ned Jarrett, Lenoir-Rhyne College; Ann Landers, Duke University; Johnny Cash, Gardner-Webb University; Bill Cosby, UNC-Pembroke.

**5**

True. It was the Augusta-area address of Jeeter Lester in Erskine Caldwell's scandalous 1932 novel by that name.

**6**

One in eight.

**7**

Wendell, after Oliver Wendell Holmes (although Holmes might have been surprised to hear it pronounced "Win-DELL").

**8**

Because of miscommunication, the finished painting, 17' × 19', was too large for its assigned 8' × 10' space. The state backed out of the deal, and Sully eventually sold the painting to the Boston Museum of Fine Arts.

**9**

"Education."

**10**

Society columnist at the *News and Observer*.

**11**

All have visited Wingate University in Union County as part of the Jesse Helms Lecture Series.

**12**

Ninety thousand.

**13**

Norman Thomas, perennial Socialist Party presidential candidate.

**14**

Richard M. Nixon, in 1936.

**15**

Princeton of the South, Davidson College; Paris of the South, Asheville; Chicago of the South, Durham; Mouth of the South, ACC basketball announcer Bill Currie.

**16**

True.

**17**

*Cold Mountain,* by Raleigh's Charles Frazier. Published in 1997, it won the National Book

Award for fiction and sold more than a million copies in hardback.

**18**

Raleigh.

**19**

Maya Angelou, most recently professor at Wake Forest University. She changed her name in the mid-1950s while touring Europe and Africa as an entertainer.

**20**

Guilford College, New Garden Boarding School; N.C. State University, N.C. College of Agricultural and Mechanic Arts; N.C. Central University, N.C. College for Negroes; UNC-Greensboro, Woman's College.

**21**

UNC-Pembroke. Its student body today is about 25 percent Native American.

**22**

Clyde Edgerton. *Raney,* his 1985 novel, won appreciative reviews for its droll depiction of life in eastern North Carolina but angered the Campbell administration. Edgerton eventually resigned.

**23**

Davidson College. Styron left after a "miserable" freshman year and eventually graduated from Duke.

**24**

Alamance County.

**25**

Outsider or visionary art. Simpson builds towering whirligigs from scrap metal; Jones chainsaws animals from tree stumps; Jennings designs smaller-scale works with titles such as *Bad Girl Goes to Hell and Beats Hell out of the Devil* (based on a story he read in the *National Enquirer*).

**26**

*Shoe*, in which the title character is modeled after Jim Shumaker, who taught cartoonist Jeff MacNelly in the late 1960s.

**27**

Davidson, which began accepting women in 1973.

**28**

Harry Golden, editor of Charlotte's *Carolina Israelite* and author of *Only in America* and *For Two Cents Plain*.

**29**

Two.

**30**

Betty Smith of Chapel Hill, author of *A Tree Grows in Brooklyn*.

**31**

Booker T. Washington, founder of Tuskegee Institute in Alabama. In 1903 African Americans in Scotland County wrote a letter telling Washington that they were provided only with an elementary school education and pleading with him to send teachers to start a school. He dispatched newlyweds Emanuel and Tinny

McDuffie (he was eighteen, she seventeen) and they built Laurinburg Institute from scratch.

**32**

Robert Ruark, Wilmington native, University of North Carolina alumnus (class of 1935), and syndicated newspaper columnist.

**33**

Sarah and Elizabeth Delany (authors of *Having Our Say: The Delany Sisters' First 100 Years*), St. Augustine's; Earl Monroe (basketball player), Winston-Salem State; Dan Blue (first black speaker of the N.C. House), N.C. Central; Ron McNair (*Challenger* astronaut), North Carolina A&T.

**34**

*The Second Coming,* by University of North Carolina alumnus Walker Percy (class of 1937).

**35**

Conover, after Antonio Canova, whose marble statue of George Washington was destroyed in the Capitol fire of 1831, then copied and reinstalled in 1970.

**36**

Trinidad.

**37**

Fresco painting on wet plaster. Since 1973 Statesville native Ben Long, who studied the form in Italy, has completed six frescoes in Charlotte, Glendale Springs, and Beaver Creek.

**38**

New Bern, mostly in the 1940s.

**39**

In Greensboro, Gen. Nathanael Greene, Revolutionary War hero; in Winston-Salem, R. J. Reynolds, tobacco industrialist.

**40**

*Mississippi: The Closed Society.* Silver's speech received national attention, although the influential *Clarion-Ledger* in Jackson ran only a brief report that he had "abused the state of Mississippi, its people, officials and newspapers in the same fashion he has in previous speeches."

**41**

Barbara Howar.

**42**

Joseph Mitchell, who arrived in New York City from Fairmont the day after the crash of 1929 and went on to become, in the words of an appreciation in the *Virginia Quarterly Review,* "unofficial poet laureate of the nation's Sodom." His work for the *New Yorker* lasted from 1937 until 1964.

**43**

*Primary Colors,* by "Anonymous," based on Bill Clinton's 1992 presidential campaign. Despite his earlier denials, "Anonymous" turned out to be *Newsweek* columnist Joe Klein.

**44**

Henry James.

**45**

Lee Smith, *Fair and Tender Ladies;* Allen Gurganus, *Oldest Living Confederate Widow;* Gail Godwin, *Father Melancholy's Daughter;*

T. R. Pearson, *Short History of a Small Place;*
Kaye Gibbons, *Ellen Foster.*

**46**

1900. Lamenting the state's puny literary out-
put, Mary Oates Van Landingham asked the
Mecklenburg Historical Society: "Could it be
that being located between Virginia and South
Carolina, our people for so long have been
furnished such conspicuous illustrations of
self-appreciation that they have, by contrast,
learned modesty and silence? Where there
are mountains of conceit, there are apt to be
valleys of humility."

**47**

Marion Hargrove, who was twenty-three years
old when *See Here, Private Hargrove* hit No. 1
in 1942, the list's first year. The book, based on
Hargrove's World War II letters home from Fort
Bragg to the *Charlotte News,* sold 3.5 million
copies and was later made into a movie.

**48**

None. When the museum opened in 1956, it
claimed five works by Rembrandt in its collection. Over the years, however, all have been
attributed to other artists of his time.

**49**

John Shelton Reed, author of such works as *My
Tears Spoiled My Aim, Whistling Dixie,* and
(with his wife, Dale Volberg Reed) *1001 Things
Everyone Should Know about the South.*

**50**

The Vietnam Veterans Memorial in Washington, D.C.

## 51

Ruth Graham, wife of evangelist Billy Graham. Cornwell was a close friend of the Grahams while growing up in Montreat.

## 52

Willem de Kooning.

## 53

Poet laureate of North Carolina.

## 54

The Cape Hatteras Lighthouse.

## 55

Thomas Dixon (1864–1946), author of *The Clansman,* the novel that became *Birth of a Nation,* and W. J. Cash (1900–1941), author of *The Mind of the South.*

## 56

The Dorton Arena, which architect Matthew Nowicki designed around two enormous, opposing concrete arches.

## 57

Gertrude Stein. Etta and her sister Claribel were close friends of the writer, until Alice B. Toklas came between them.

## 58

*Inside U.S.A.,* by journalist John Gunther.

## 59

Storytelling, especially Appalachian versions of the ancient Jack Tales, in which a poor but virtuous boy survives by his wits, as in "Jack and the Beanstalk."

**60**

*Blue Highways: A Journey into America.*
William Least Heat Moon did find the site of
his ancestor's grave, near Asheboro, but it had
recently been covered by a reservoir.

**61**

Robert Frost. Almost seventy years later, he
would tell a biographer, "I suppose it was all
nothing but my young way of having the blues."

**62**

Eli Evans. In *The Provincials,* Evans writes,
"I am not certain what it means to be both a
Jew and a Southerner . . . to have inherited the
Jewish longing for a homeland, while raised
with the Southerner's sense of home."

**63**

Thomas Wolfe (1900–1938) and O. Henry
(1862–1910). O. Henry, whose real name was
William Sydney Porter, was born in Greensboro.

**64**

Frederick Law Olmsted, then a correspondent for the *New York Times,* later a famed
landscape architect.

**65**

Blowing Rock, where novelist Jan Karon has
written *At Home in Mitford, A Light in the
Window, These High Green Hills,* and *Out to
Caanan.*

**66**

The North Carolina School of the Arts, awarded
to Winston-Salem in 1964. Among its alumni:
actor Tom Hulce (*Amadeus*), actress Mary-

Louise Parker (*Fried Green Tomatoes*),
actor-singer-dancer Terrence Mann (*Cats*),
and actor-director Joe Montello (*Angels in
America*).

**67**

Anne Tyler, who went on to become a Pulitzer
Prize–winning novelist. Tyler was born in Min-
neapolis but graduated from Broughton High
School in Raleigh and then Duke University.

**68**

The family would have preferred that the
$68,000 raised for the statue be spent on
projects of its own choosing. The statue was
also widely criticized for its lack of resemblance
to King.

**69**

North Carolina State University; the University
of North Carolina at Chapel Hill ranks second.

**70**

*Uncle Tom's Cabin,* by Harriet Beecher Stowe.

**71**

Mathew Brady, whose Civil War photos would
become world famous. "I yielded to the request
of an artist named Brady, of New York, by
sitting for my daguerreotype likeness today,"
Polk wrote in his diary. "I sat in the large
dining-room."

**72**

Reynolds Price, who encountered Clinton on an
elevator while attending a White House dinner.
Clinton memorized the line from *A Long and
Happy Life* as a teenager. (It begins, "Just
with his body and from inside like a snake,

leaning that black motorcycle side to side, cutting in and out of the slow line of cars to get there first, staring due-north through goggles towards Mount Moriah and switching coon tails in everybody's face was Wesley Beavers.")

**73**

Fayetteville's Bragg Boulevard.

**74**

East Carolina University, which was East Carolina Teachers College until 1951.

**75**

French science fiction pioneer Jules Verne, who set *The Master of the World* (1904) atop a mountain near Morganton.

**76**

Davidson College. Rusk and Foster graduated from Davidson, but Wilson transferred to Princeton after his freshman year.

**77**

It's the oldest, founded by Moravian settlers in 1772.

**78**

Jack Kerouac. *Visions of Gerard* would be poorly received, but *On the Road,* which was still without a publisher during Kerouac's visit, would soon ensure his fame. Still standing at the town's West Mount crossroads is the frame house where he stayed.

**79**

Jerry Bledsoe of Asheboro, bestselling author of *Bitter Blood, Blood Games,* and *Before He Wakes.*

**80**

Ferlinghetti, who was circulation manager. The future Beat Generation poet and publisher, a native of Yonkers, New York, chose UNC out of admiration for Thomas Wolfe. At Chapel Hill he went by Larry Ferling.

**81**

Kurt Vonnegut.

# COMMERCE AND SCIENCE

*There is not a man whose residence is in the State who is recognized by the world as an authority on anything. Since time began no man nor woman who lived there has ever written a book that has taken a place in the permanent literature of the country. Not a man has ever lived and worked there who fills twenty-five pages in any history of the United States. Not a scientific discovery has been made and worked out and kept its home in North Carolina that ever became famous for the good it did the world. It is the laughing stock among the States.*

*Editor and future diplomat Walter Hines Page, in an 1886 letter to the* State Chronicle *in Raleigh, goading the legislature to at last authorize what will become North Carolina State University*


*Henry Ford had to start somewheres.*

*Taylorsville inventor Gerald Warren in 1983, revealing his plans for a perpetual-motion air car*

# QUESTIONS

**1**

True or false: North Carolina is the nation's leading producer of yams.

**2**

Match the restaurant chain with its hometown:

| | |
|---|---|
| Biscuitville | Raleigh |
| Bojangles' | Claremont |
| Golden Corral | Charlotte |
| Western Steer | Graham |

**3**

Wilmington to Charlotte to Cincinnati was the inaugural route of what airline?

**4**

True or false: North Carolina's work force is the least unionized of any state in the nation.

**5**

In what year did surgeons at Duke University Medical Center perform North Carolina's first successful heart transplant: 1965, 1975, or 1985?

**6**

What familiar product is named for Charlotte native Herman Lay: Oil of Olay, the La-Z-Boy recliner, or Lay's Potato Chips?

**7**

In 1799 twelve-year-old Conrad Reed brought home a seventeen-pound gold nugget he had found while fishing in a Cabarrus County stream. It would be three years, however, before his find set off the Carolina Gold Rush. Why?

**8**

The first discovery of this metal in the United States was made near Lexington in 1838. What was it?

**9**

In TV commercials in the early 1970s, who sang, "Hurry on down to Hardee's, where the burgers are charcoal-broiled"?

**10**

What governor, jumping at *Life* magazine's invitation to promote the state's industries in a photo spread, took a shower fully clothed "in quick-drying synthetic fabrics made in North Carolina"?

**11**

North Carolina's first sales tax, enacted in 1933, exempted nine foods. What were they?

**12**

The celebrated Sotheby's auction of items from her estate included a tray presented to Jacqueline Kennedy during a visit to Charlotte with her husband, then a U.S. senator. Was the selling price closer to $250, $25,000, or $250,000?

**13**

What is Mother Vineyard?

**14**

According to Peter Applebome's 1996 book *Dixie Rising: How the South Is Shaping American Values, Politics, and Culture,* this city "may edge out Dallas and Atlanta as home of the purest strain ever discovered of the Southern booster gene. [It] has Dallas's hustle and go-go sense of civic unanimity without its meanness, and it has Atlanta's leafy geography and optimism without the worst of its big-city problems and insufferable sense of triumphalism." What city is it?

**15**

True or false: Flue-cured bright-leaf tobacco, used in cigarettes, is typically grown in eastern North Carolina. Burley tobacco, used in cigars, pipe tobacco, and cigarette blends, is grown in western North Carolina.

**16**

New Orleans's "Streetcar Named Desire," made famous by playwright Tennessee Williams, was built in what city?

**17**

What newspaper refused to publish a 1988 *Doonesbury* installment depicting an R. J. Reynolds job applicant who is unable to say, "Cigarettes do not cause cancer," without laughing?

**18**

Do more hogs or people live in North Carolina?

**19**

Some four hundred workers, most of them misdemeanor convicts, died in what 1870s construction project?

**20**

When it opened in 1949, it was the South's largest shopping center. What was it?

**21**

Before tobacco, what was North Carolina's No. 1 crop?

**22**

What was the purpose of the state's first railroad, built in Raleigh in 1833?

**23**

North Carolina's first McDonald's opened in 1959 in what city?

**24**

Name the six passenger trains that operate in North Carolina.

**25**

The influenza epidemic of 1918 proved a boon to what North Carolina product?

**26**

Which of these is the state's oldest continuously published daily newspaper: the *Fayetteville Observer,* the *Salisbury Post,* or the *Wilmington Morning Star?*

**27**

Before his flight to Paris, Charles Lindbergh offered to name his plane after what North Carolina product?

**28**

The New York Racket, on Main Street in Monroe, was the first store opened by what future retail magnate?

**29**

In what year did Charlotte become the first city in the South to fluoridate its water: 1909, 1929, or 1949?

**30**

During the national bank holiday decreed by Franklin Roosevelt in 1933, the Bank of Englehard continued doing business as usual. Why?

**31**

The first cotton mill in the South began production in 1813. Was it near Lincolnton, Lenoir, or Lexington?

**32**

The largest tobacco market in the country is in what city: Richmond, Va.; Lexington, Ky.; or Wilson, N.C.?

**33**

True or false: The sixty-eight-foot-wide dome at UNC–Chapel Hill's Morehead Planetarium is the largest in the United States.

**34**

What city for many years billed itself as "renowned the world around"?

**35**

True or false: Charlotte/Douglas International is the state's busiest airport, but three out of four passengers are only changing planes there.

**36**

A 1962 article in what magazine gave North Carolina the laudatory label of "Dixie Dynamo"?

**37**

The longest straight railroad track in the United States, extending seventy-eight miles, links the longtime rail hub of Hamlet with what city?

**38**

What network news personality testified in a Greensboro courtroom in 1997?

**39**

What North Carolina consumer product inspired an enduring, if corny, telephone prank?

**40**

What small but controversial change in in-flight service did USAir (now US Airways) make after purchasing Piedmont Airlines in 1987?

**41**

What basic laboratory device was perfected in 1887 by UNC–Chapel Hill chemistry professor Francis Venable?

**42**

The original area code for North Carolina, 704, was established in what year: 1947, 1957, or 1967?

**43**

After Thomasville (Chair City) built the "world's largest chair" in 1922, how did High Point (Furniture City) respond?

**44**

In 1998 scientists found what new possible cause of the disappearance of the Lost Colony?

**45**

What site on the North Carolina coast served as a secret test range in the early days of the U.S. missile program?

**46**

Name the nine North Carolina companies that made the Fortune 500 announced in 1999.

**47**

In the North Carolina mountains, what lucrative commodity is known as "sang"?

**48**

Before settling on "Camels," R. J. Reynolds almost named his new brand of cigarettes after what world leader?

**49**

How did the Wright Brothers decide which of the two would have first chance at piloting their prototype flying machine at Kill Devil Hills?

**50**

Among the failed early ventures of this future fast-food pioneer was a motel and restaurant in Asheville that opened in 1939 and closed a couple of years later. Who was he?

**51**

How did Midway Airlines, based at Raleigh-Durham International, get its name?

**52**

Which of the following statements about Sylva native Dr. John Brinkley (1885–1942) are true?

He was labeled a "giant in quackery" by the American Medical Association.

At his Brinkley Gland Hospital in Milford,

Kansas, he transplanted goat glands into impotent men (cost: $750) and set up a radio station to promote his practice.

Shut down by the FCC, Brinkley retaliated with a write-in campaign for governor of Kansas and almost won.

One of his mail-order elixirs, Crazy Water Crystals, sponsor of WBT's *Briarhoppers* show, was shown to be a horse laxative.

## 53

How did Pinehurst founder James Walker Tufts make his fortune?

## 54

What Gaston County town is named for the British engineer who discovered how to make steel from cast iron?

## 55

What was the world-renowned innovation of Duke University's Dr. Walter Kempner?

## 56

The "Big Three" headache powders all originated in North Carolina. Name the products and their hometowns.

## 57

For what was L. A. "Speed" Riggs famous?

## 58

Although the violent Loray Mill strike in Gastonia in 1929 made news around the world, there is no historic marker commemorating it. Why?

## 59

Which of these originated in North Carolina: Morse code, the Code of Hammurabi, "Omerta" (the Mafia's code of silence), or the Universal Product Code?

## 60

What was Black Wall Street?

## 61

On December 18, 1903, the *Norfolk Virginian-Pilot* scooped the world with a front-page story headlined "FLYING MACHINE SOARS THREE MILES IN TEETH OF HIGH WIND OVER SAND HILLS AND WAVES AT KITTY HAWK ON CAROLINA COAST." Remarkably, the epochal account would make hardly a ripple. Why?

## 62

What was the original product sold by Lance, the Charlotte snack food manufacturer?

## 63

Over the years, what city has been shown by market surveys to lead the nation in per-capita consumption of catsup, Spam, and Beanee Weenee?

## 64

What North Carolina town is named after the first American to undertake an international advertising campaign?

## 65

Which of these men of letters never endorsed Bull Durham tobacco: Alfred Lord Tennyson, Thomas Carlyle, James Russell Lowell, or Henry David Thoreau?

## 66

How did Winston industrialist P. H. Hanes get started in the men's underwear business?

**67**

What North Carolina town is named for
the industrialist who coined the term "air
conditioning"?

**68**

One of the oldest and most popular exhibits
at the North Carolina Museum of Natural
Sciences is nicknamed "Trouble." What is it?

**69**

We leave our home in the morning,
We kiss our children good-bye,
While we slave for the bosses,
Our children scream and cry.

. . . . . . . . . . .

But understand, all workers,
Our union they do fear.
Let's stand together, workers,
And have a union here.

These lines come from a ballad written by what
martyred labor organizer?

**70**

"Conceived by Genius, achieved by Dauntless
Resolution and Unconquerable Faith." What
achievement do these words commemorate?

**71**

In 1934, Dr. J. B. Rhine of Duke University
startled the scientific world with a paper
detailing experiments in which a student
guessed what symbols were on cards being
dealt face-down by a research assistant in
another campus building. The title of Rhine's
paper quickly became a household word. What
was it?

**72**

What are terpenes and what do they have to do with the Blue Ridge Mountains?

**73**

How did Kansas developers Samuel Kelsey and Charles Hutchinson choose a site for the summer resort they were planning in 1875?

**74**

The nation's largest deposits of this versatile ore are extracted from open-pit mines in Cleveland and Gaston Counties. What is it?

**75**

*GQ* magazine referred to it as "the Appalachian love child of the soufflé and the croissant." Nora Ephron, writing in the *New Yorker*, called it "light as a frosted snowflake." North Carolinians know it by what name?

**76**

What influential 1997 book accused state government of mishandling research on pfiesteria, a tiny, toxic organism preying on fish in the rivers of eastern North Carolina?

**77**

Replacements Ltd. in Greensboro is the world's largest retailer of what?

**78**

Mexican Joe was the original name of what familiar tabletop condiment?

**79**

Who were "Sunglasses," "Saxophone," "Microphone," and "Hands"?

**80**

After World War II, three industries accounted for 70 percent of all factory jobs in the state. By the 1990s their share had fallen to less than 40 percent. What were these Big Three?

**81**

Hiddenite in Alexander County is North America's top source of what gemstones?

**82**

True or false: In 1900 North Carolina produced more wine than any other state.

**83**

Henry Petroski, a Duke University engineering professor, won acclaim in 1990 for his 450-page book on what common household item?

**84**

Television celebrity Dinah Shore was spokeswoman for what North Carolina product during the 1980s?

**85**

In 1972 the owner of a struggling Charlotte UHF station staged a successful telethon to keep it on the air. Who was he?

**86**

Glen Raven Mills holds what distinction in women's fashion history?

**87**

McLean Stevenson, who played Col. Henry Blake on the TV series *M*A*S*H*, was spokesman for what North Carolina company during the 1980s?

**88**

What is the best-known product of P&P Chair Company in Asheboro?

**89**

What are the best-known products of Charlotte's Radiator Specialty Company?

**90**

What revolutionary product did Hanes Hosiery of Winston-Salem introduce in 1971?

**91**

In 1987 Kivett's Inc. of Clinton, one of the nation's largest manufacturers of sanctuary seating, designed and donated an ornate, six-hundred-pound, bulletproof oak chair for a famous visitor to the United States. Who was he?

**92**

From about 1720 to 1870, North Carolina led the world in the production of "naval stores." What are they?

**93**

What well-known food processor is located at the corner of Cucumber and Vine Streets?

**94**

The state's first long-distance telephone call, in 1879, linked Western Union offices in what two cities?

**95**

The first use of an X ray in North Carolina occurred in Charlotte in 1896. What object did it enable a physician to retrieve from the throat of a little girl?

**96**

Match these products with their hometowns:

| | |
|---|---|
| Slim Jim sausages | Salisbury |
| Red Bird peppermint candy | Garner |
| Cheerwine soda pop | Edenton |
| Jimbo's Jumbos peanuts | Lexington |

**97**

After seven hundred Mary Kay beauty consultants set the ballroom vibrating and sent insulation falling onto an Amway convention below, the Charlotte Convention Center banned what activity?

# ANSWERS

**1**

False. It is, however, No. 1 in sweet potatoes. Yams are grown mostly in South America, the Caribbean, and western Africa and have white, barklike flesh. Most people, however, have come to use the names interchangeably for the southern orange-fleshed root.

**2**

Biscuitville, Graham; Bojangles', Charlotte; Golden Corral, Raleigh; Western Steer, Claremont.

**3**

Piedmont Airlines, which began DC-3 service in 1948. Over the next four decades, Piedmont, headquartered in Winston-Salem, grew from a "puddle jumper" operation to the nation's eighth-largest airline before being merged into USAir.

**4**

False. As of 1998, North Carolina was forty-ninth, with a 3.8 percent unionization rate, just ahead of South Carolina at 3.7 percent. The national average is 14.1 percent.

**5**

1985. The patient was fifty-five-year-old Thomas Harrison, a Durham plumber.

**6**

Lay's Potato Chips.

**7**

His father, not recognizing it as gold, used it as a doorstop until offering it to a Fayetteville jeweler for $3.50.

**8**

Silver.

**9**

Mama Cass Elliot, formerly of the Mamas and the Papas.

**10**

Luther Hodges, in 1956.

**11**

Flour, cornmeal, meat, lard, milk, molasses, salt, sugar, and coffee.

**12**

$25,000. The eight-inch-diameter electroplated salver was monogrammed with the initials of Jacqueline Lee Bouvier Kennedy and inscribed, "From the Charlotte Chamber of Commerce, Jan. 15, 1959."

**13**

The oldest scuppernong vine in the country. Some historians say Indians on Roanoke Island planted the vine more than five hundred years ago; others credit early colonists. Regardless, the vineyard – now reduced to a single, nonproducing vine – was responsible for the nation's first cultivated wine grape.

**14**

Charlotte.

## 15

True.

## 16

High Point. The Perley A. Thomas Car Works supplied New Orleans with more than a hundred streetcars, some of which remain in service today.

## 17

The *Winston-Salem Journal*.

## 18

Hogs, by an approximate count of 10 million to 7.4 million.

## 19

Bringing the railroad westward through the mountains to Asheville. The Swannanoa Tunnel alone claimed 120 lives in 1879.

## 20

Cameron Village in Raleigh.

## 21

Cotton. Though much of the state's soil was poorly suited to grow it, cotton was so profitable that in 1926, its peak year, North Carolina farmers planted 1.8 million acres.

## 22

The temporary, mile-long line hauled granite from a quarry to the site of the new state capitol. On Sundays it took passengers on outings.

## 23

Greensboro.

**24**

The Carolinian, the Crescent, the Piedmont, the Silver Star, the Silver Meteor, and the Silver Palm.

**25**

Vick's VapoRub, a menthol salve manufactured in Greensboro.

**26**

The *Wilmington Morning Star,* founded in 1867.

**27**

Lucky Strike cigarettes. American Tobacco, leery of a possible crash, said "no thanks" to the sponsorship deal, and Lindbergh went instead with the Spirit of St. Louis.

**28**

William Henry Belk, in 1888. The Belk department store chain now comprises about 225 stores across the South.

**29**

1949.

**30**

Word of the presidential order never reached the remote Hyde County fishing village.

**31**

Lincolnton. Founded by Michael Schenck, a Pennsylvania-born merchant, the mill was a forerunner of the textile industry that would eventually center in nearby Gaston County.

**32**

Wilson.

**33**

False. That distinction belongs to the seventy-nine-foot dome at the Kelly Space Voyager Planetarium at Discovery Place in Charlotte.

**34**

Durham, as a result of the widespread use of Bull Durham tobacco.

**35**

True, thanks to US Airways' use of Charlotte as a "hub" airport.

**36**

*National Geographic.*

**37**

Wilmington.

**38**

Diane Sawyer of ABC's *PrimeTime Live,* defending the show's use of hidden cameras in reporting unsanitary practices at Food Lion grocery stores. The jury awarded Food Lion $5.5 million in punitive damages, but a judge reduced this amount to $315,000, and ABC continues to appeal the verdict.

**39**

Prince Albert pipe tobacco, manufactured by R. J. Reynolds from 1909 until 1987. The caller would ask the storekeeper, "Do you have Prince Albert in a can?" An affirmative answer brought the punchline: "Well, you'd better let him out!"

**40**

It dropped Piedmont's policy of serving passengers a full can of soda, instead offering only a six-ounce cup. USAir initially yielded to a wave of complaints about its chintziness but finally dropped full-can service for good during a 1993 cost-cutting campaign.

**41**

The Bunsen burner.

**42**

1947. In 1954 the eastern part of the state was assigned the 919 code, and by 1999 the state had been further subdivided into six area codes.

**43**

By building the "world's largest bureau," a simulated chest of drawers that would house a visitor center and the Chamber of Commerce.

**44**

The worst drought in eight hundred years, as determined from the rings of ancient bald cypress trees.

**45**

Topsail Island, in the late 1940s.

**46**

In order, largest first: Bank of America, First Union, Duke Energy, Lowe's, Wachovia, VF, Nucor, Carolina Power and Light, and BB&T.

**47**

Ginseng, valued as a tonic. The wild herb's gnarled roots, dug up with sharpened sticks, are commonly exported to Asia.

**48**

Kaiser Wilhelm II of Germany. Reynolds was saved by his second thoughts: "I don't think we should name a product for a living man.

You can never tell what the damn fool will do."
Indeed, the kaiser's war broke out in Europe
soon after Camels hit the market in 1913.

## 49

Wilbur Wright won a coin toss with brother
Orville. The first flight lasted 3½ seconds.

## 50

Colonel Harland Sanders. He thought he could
repeat the success of his Sanders Court in
Corbin, Ky., but a combination of wartime
rationing, stiff local competition, and tourist-
poor winters proved insurmountable.

## 51

Before filing for bankruptcy and relocating in
1995, it had operated out of Chicago's Midway
Airport.

## 52

All are true.

## 53

He developed the soda fountain.

## 54

Bessemer City. Local iron deposits proved dis-
appointing, however, and by the 1900s textiles
had become the town's dominant industry.

## 55

The Rice Diet, a low-fat, low-salt rice and fruit
regimen that lowers blood pressure and choles-
terol. Since 1939, more than 22,000 "Ricers,"
including celebrities from Jimmy Durante to
Jimmy "the Greek" Snyder, have participated
in the program.

**56**

Goody's, Winston-Salem; BC, Durham; Stan-
back, Salisbury.

**57**

For thirty-three years, the former Goldsboro
tobacco auctioneer pitched American
Tobacco's Lucky Strikes on the radio with a
singsong chant that ended "Sold, American!"

**58**

The N.C. Division of Archives and History and
the city have never been able to agree on an
inscription. In 1987 Gastonia's mayor and city
council rejected the state's proposal: "A strike
in 1929 at Loray Mill . . . left two dead and
spurred opposition to labor unions statewide."
They preferred, "In a 1929 strike at Loray
Mill . . . local citizens defeated first communist
efforts to control southern textiles."

**59**

The Universal Product Code. The UPC "bar
code" was invented in 1973 by George Laurer,
a senior engineer at IBM's Research Triangle
Park facility.

**60**

A row of banks and insurance companies on
Parrish Street in segregated downtown Durham. Best known was North Carolina Mutual
Life Insurance, the nation's largest black-owned
business.

**61**

Less than two weeks before, Samuel Lang-
ley, head of the Smithsonian Institution, had
met with ignominious and widely publicized
failure when his Great Aerodrome crashed

into the Potomac River, almost killing the pilot
and plunging the credibility of flying-machine
builders to an all-time low.

**62**

Peanuts. In 1913 Charlotte coffee salesman
Phillip Lance found himself stuck with five hundred pounds of peanuts he had ordered for a
farmer who changed his mind. In desperation,
Lance roasted the peanuts in his home oven
and sold them in bags. In the 1920s, Lance
began making peanut butter and spreading it
on crackers.

**63**

Charlotte.

**64**

Carrboro. By the 1880s, Julian Shakespeare
Carr had used newspaper ads, store cards,
and outdoor signs to make his Bull Durham
tobacco "renowned the world around." In 1913
the Orange County town of Venable changed
its name to Carrboro to honor one of its biggest
employers.

**65**

Henry David Thoreau.

**66**

He invested the proceeds from selling his plug-
tobacco company to rival R. J. Reynolds in
1900.

**67**

Cramerton in Gaston County. In a 1906 speech
to the Southern Cotton Manufacturers' Association convention in Asheville, Stuart Cramer
discussed his pioneering "air-conditioning"

system in the Gray Manufacturing plant in
Gastonia.

**68**

The skeleton of a fifty-five-foot-long sperm
whale that washed onto Wrightsville Beach
in 1928. "Trouble," as it was dubbed by nose-
holding townspeople, lay in the sun for more
than a week before museum curators came to
the rescue and hauled it to Raleigh.

**69**

Ella May Wiggins, mother of five, who was shot
from ambush on the way to a union rally during
the violent 1929 strike at Gastonia's Loray
Mill. At her funeral, a mourner sang Wiggins's
ballad, titled "Mill Mother's Lament."

**70**

The Wright brothers' flight at Kitty Hawk. The
words are part of an inscription on a granite
monument at the Wright Brothers National
Memorial.

**71**

"Extra-sensory Perception," popularly short-
ened to ESP.

**72**

They're chemicals given off by coniferous trees,
and they're responsible for the characteristic
haze that gives the Blue Ridge its name.

**73**

On a map they drew one line from Chicago to
Savannah and another from Baltimore to New
Orleans. Where the lines intersected, they built
Highlands.

**74**

Lithium, used in products from nuclear weapons to medicine for bipolar (or manic-depressive) disorder.

**75**

The Krispy Kreme doughnut, introduced in Winston-Salem in 1937 but virtually unknown in New York until 1996.

**76**

*And the Waters Turned to Blood,* by Rodney Barker.

**77**

Discontinued china, crystal, and flatware. Bob Page began the business in 1981 as an outgrowth of his weekend hobby.

**78**

Texas Pete hot sauce, concocted by Thad W. Garner in 1929 and still manufactured in Winston-Salem.

**79**

The original four California Raisin figures distributed by Hardee's in 1987 to promote its cinnamon raisin biscuits. The Rocky Mount–based hamburger chain eventually sold more than fifty million Raisins and doubled its breakfast sales.

**80**

Textiles, tobacco, and furniture.

**81**

Emeralds.

**82**

True. Within a few years, however, prohibition closed North Carolina's scuppernong vineyards, and the industry would never return to its former prominence.

**83**

The pencil, in *The Pencil: A History of Design and Circumstance.*

**84**

Holly Farms chicken, processed in Wilkesboro.

**85**

Future media magnate Ted Turner. Turner later repaid contributors with 6 percent interest before selling WRET (for Robert E. Turner) to Westinghouse Broadcasting Company for $20 million.

**86**

It was the original manufacturer of pantyhose. The idea evolved from the stretch tights already being made by the mill in Glen Raven in Alamance County. Company president Allen Gant discussed with his wife the concept of sewing a pair of sheer stockings to a pair of underpants. After she test-wore the patched-together garment, designers refined the idea. Panti-Legs, trademarked in 1960, took off with the popularity of the miniskirt. Among the satisfied customers: fan dancer Sally Rand, who sent the company a photograph of herself wearing Panti-Legs and a letter explaining how she adapted them to her dance routine.

**87**

Piedmont Airlines.

## 88

The Carolina Rocker, unofficially known as "the Kennedy Rocker." To ease his chronically sore back, President Kennedy purchased one of the Appalachian red oak chairs from P&P in 1955. Kennedy's attachment to the chair – he even took it aboard Air Force One – made it world famous. In 1996 one of the several rockers in his collection fetched $453,500 at Sotheby's Jacqueline Kennedy Onassis estate auction.

## 89

Solder Seal, Gunk, and Liquid Wrench.

## 90

L'eggs pantyhose, sold in supermarkets and drugstores in a plastic, egg-shaped container. Previously, pantyhose came stretched over leg-shaped cardboard inserts and required a trip to a department store. The eggs won numerous design awards before being quietly phased out in the late 1980s.

## 91

Pope John Paul II, who sat in the chair during his stop in Detroit.

## 92

Tar, pitch, and turpentine, used to seal and preserve wooden ships.

## 93

Mt. Olive Pickle Company. Mt. Olive ranks second to Vlasic as the largest-selling shelf pickle brand in the country.

## 94

Raleigh and Wilmington.

**95**

A thimble.

**96**

Slim Jims, Garner; Red Bird, Lexington; Cheerwine, Salisbury; Jimbo's, Edenton.

**97**

Bunny hopping.

# THE CULTURE

*A custom prevalent in North Carolina [is] the women chewing tobacco . . . in a most disgusting and disagreeable way, if one way can be more disgusting than another. They carry habitually a small stick . . . in their glove, or their garter string, and, whenever occasion offers, plunge it into a snuffbox, and begin chewing it. The practice is so common, that the proffer of the snuffbox, and its passing from hand to hand, is the usual civility of a morning visit among the country people.*

*English actress Fanny Kemble, en route from Philadelphia to Georgia by stagecoach in 1838, recoiling at what she observes in "the poorest state in the Union"*

*We just got the wrong mix of people. We had God-fearing, flag-waving, red-white-and-blue folks out there with the motorcycle boys.*

*H. A. "Humpy" Wheeler, Charlotte Motor Speedway president, reflecting on the fights that erupted when a Waylon Jennings concert was scheduled on qualifying day for the World 600 in 1980; in the melee, 8 people were injured, 3 were arrested, and 175 riot police were called out.*

# QUESTIONS

**1**

What innovation introduced by Warner Stamey of Greensboro in the 1950s soon became common at barbecue joints across the state?

**2**

True or false: In 1978, North Carolina's chapter of the American Cancer Society was the only one in the country not to support the Great American Smoke-out.

**3**

About one of his floor speeches, the *New York Times* predicted, "It will contain much vulgarity and much that a Senator of this generation ought to be ashamed of, but it will not be dull." To whom was the *Times* referring?

**4**

What descendants of the 1960s counterculture held their 1987 "Gathering of the Tribes" in the Nantahala National Forest outside Robbinsville, creating a major public health problem?

**5**

A longtime congressman from North Carolina and a PBS talk show host from North Carolina share a name. What is it?

and painting Durham as "a flat-out dump . . . grubby, ramshackle, depressing"?

## 22

The Biltmore House has thirty-four master bedrooms. What was the greatest number of Vanderbilt family members to live there at one time?

## 23

True or false: *New York Times* food writer Craig Claiborne declared Texas beef barbecue superior to North Carolina pork barbecue.

## 24

In 1940 North Carolina was the nation's eleventh-most-populous state. Where did it rank in farm population?

## 25

The Union forces that captured New Bern during the Civil War were led by a man more widely remembered today for his contribution to the lexicon. Who was he?

## 26

In 1949 Harvard historian V. O. Key described twentieth-century North Carolina as being governed by which of these: a "progressive plutocracy," a "regressive republic," or an "obstreperous oligarchy"?

## 27

True or false: In 1957 Wilmington became the first North Carolina city since World War II to switch to daylight-savings time, but its county, New Hanover, remained on standard time.

**28**

Nearly one-third of North Carolina's Lumbee Indians have one of what two surnames?

**29**

Match the bridegroom with the place where he married:

| | |
|---|---|
| Horace Greeley, newspaper editor | Greensboro |
| Charlton Heston, actor | Warrenton |
| Walter Reed, physician | Murfreesboro |
| Stephen Douglas, debater of Abraham Lincoln | Rockingham County |

**30**

In 1928 the *University of North Carolina Newsletter* reported that, in less than a decade, the state population of what animal had fallen from 171,000 to 105,000?

**31**

True or false: North Carolina law prohibits restaurants from serving "barbecue" that hasn't been cooked over an open pit.

**32**

In a 1951 magazine article, sociologist Vance Packard described what North Carolina county as "the bootleg capital of America"?

**33**

Hugh Ashcraft of Charlotte, a bomber pilot during World War II, inspired what enduring expression?

**34**

"Shrimp and grits" was a trademark dish of what Chapel Hill chef and restaurateur?

**35**

True or false: A survey by UNC–Chapel Hill researchers showed that, between 1982 and 1992, the number of North Carolinians who considered theirs the best state to live in fell from 81 percent to 61 percent.

**36**

How did these visitors to North Carolina meet their deaths: Theodosia Burr Alston, daughter of Aaron Burr; Robert Livingstone, son of missionary David Livingstone; Blackbeard, pirate; Zelda Fitzgerald, wife of F. Scott Fitzgerald; and Sidney Lanier, poet?

**37**

When did Bob Melton of Rocky Mount open the state's first sit-down barbecue restaurant: 1904, 1924, or 1944?

**38**

Before the Revolutionary War, what was North Carolina's majority religious denomination?

**39**

True or false: Barbecue Presbyterian Church is where Rev. Will B. Dunn preaches in Doug Marlette's *Kudzu* comic strip.

**40**

According to an unsuccessful 1935 student petition opposing a proposed statue of James B. Duke, what feature of it would mark Duke University as "a gift from which the price tag has never been removed"?

**41**

What city's "public nuisance" ordinance was written up (with a three-column color photo) on the front page of the *New York Times* in 1997?

**42**

What do Pennsylvanians call the food that Piedmont North Carolinians know as livermush?

**43**

Pembroke Jones, a Wilmington rice miller and railroad heir, and his wife Sadie lived so grandly in their efforts to enter turn-of-the-century New York society that some historians believe they are the subject of a still-popular idiom. What is it?

**44**

Which of these desserts is most likely to be served at a North Carolina barbecue joint: cheesecake, strawberry shortcake, or banana pudding?

**45**

True or false: Although the expression "It's a long time between drinks," concerning a meeting between the governors of North Carolina and South Carolina, became so widely known that it was quoted by both Rudyard Kipling and Robert Louis Stevenson, it is in fact apocryphal.

# ANSWERS

**1**

Stamey added hushpuppies, already a staple at fish camps, to his menu. Before, barbecue had typically been served with white bread or rolls.

**2**

True.

**3**

Sen. Zeb Vance, in 1886. Many of Vance's anecdotes were so ribald that they were deleted from the published record.

**4**

The Rainbow Family. About half the estimated 12,000 Rainbows contracted severe shigellosis (primary symptom – diarrhea) from contaminated water, then spread it to twenty-seven states.

**5**

Charlie Rose. The television personality grew up in Warren Plains and Henderson and now owns a soybean farm in Granville County. The politician from Fayetteville served twenty-four years in the House before retiring in 1996.

**6**

William Byrd, who considered North Carolinians "slothful" and said the only reason they raised hogs was that it was so easy.

**7**

Debutantes, "looking as gracious as any antebellum belles." Inside, *Life* devoted a four-page spread to Charlotte's recent challenge to "the social supremacy" of Raleigh.

**8**

"Brown-bagging," in which restaurant patrons bought "setups" and poured their own alcohol from bottles purchased at an ABC store.

**9**

"Bunkum." During the lengthy 1820 debate over the Missouri Compromise, Walker, whose district included Buncombe County, rose to address his bored colleagues. Because his constituents expected him to say something about Missouri, Walker explained, he was compelled to "make a speech for Buncombe." The phrase "speaking for Buncombe" caught on, later abbreviated as "bunkum" and "bunk."

**10**

Jean Harlow. "As kisses go," Reynolds hastened to report, "the Hollywood variety don't compare with the homespun smacks of North Carolina."

**11**

Lexington. It's also home of the annual North Carolina Barbecue Festival.

**12**

Pennsylvania.

**13**

William Randolph Hearst, before Graham's 1949 Los Angeles crusade.

**14**

The Plott hound, a native of Haywood County known for its bear-hunting prowess.

**15**

Bob Scott, who left office in 1973, was succeeded by Jim Holshouser, Jim Hunt (two terms), Jim Martin (two terms), and Jim Hunt again (two more terms).

**16**

Cantaloupe (62 lbs., from Rocky Mount), collard (41¼" tall, from Rocky Mount), green bean (48¾" long, from Fuquay-Varina), lima bean (14" long, from Hubert), and peanut (4" long, from Enfield).

**17**

To attend the wedding of former girlfriend Frances Ann Cannon, a member of the textile family, who was marrying John Hersey, future author of *Hiroshima*.

**18**

Manteo and Wanchese, North Carolina Indians who were invited to London by explorers commissioned by Sir Walter Raleigh.

**19**

Egbert Roscoe Murrow. Born near Greensboro in 1908, Murrow hated the name Egbert and, while a student at Washington State College, went by Ed. In 1944, by now a household name on CBS radio, he filed a delayed birth certificate (none was filled out at his birth) certifying himself as Edward R. Murrow.

## 20

All once lived in Charlotte. Dowling played quarterback for the Charlotte Hornets of the World Football League; Cash sang on WBT radio as a member of the Carter Family; McGuire coached at Belmont Abbey College; Morganna stripped at the C'est Bon Club; Masters lived in retirement while his wife taught school; Brinkley operated a one-man bureau for United Press.

## 21

*GQ.*

## 22

Three.

## 23

False, of course. "I will state unequivocally that the chopped barbecue pork sandwich served in [Lexington and Goldsboro] is by far my favorite kind of barbecue," Claiborne wrote.

## 24

First.

## 25

Gen. Ambrose Burnside, whose whiskers set a new style, first as "burnsides," then as "sideburns."

## 26

A "progressive plutocracy."

## 27

True.

**28**

Oxendine and Locklear.

**29**

Greeley, Warrenton; Heston, Greensboro;
Reed, Murfreesboro; Douglas, Rockingham
County.

**30**

The horse, fast losing out to the automobile as
a means of transportation.

**31**

False. In fact, most of the state's barbecue
joints have quietly switched to gas or electricity in recent years. (Packaged for sale in
stores, however, the new-style product must be
labeled "cooked pork.")

**32**

Wilkes County.

**33**

"Coming in on a wing and a prayer." Returning
from a mission over Germany, Ashcraft's flak-
riddled B-17 was minus one engine. His remark
to his crew, "Those who want to, please pray,"
was widely publicized and turned into a hit
song.

**34**

The late Bill Neal, who made Crooks Corner a
mecca for enthusiasts of neotraditional southern cooking. "Shrimp and grits" languished on
the menu until Craig Claiborne's rave review in
the *New York Times* made it the restaurant's
most-ordered entrée.

**35**

True.

**36**

Theodosia Burr Alston was lost at sea off Cape Hatteras (1812); Robert Livingstone was killed in an escape attempt at Salisbury Prison (1864); Blackbeard was beheaded by a British naval officer at Ocracoke Inlet (1718); Zelda Fitzgerald died in a fire at a mental hospital in Asheville (1948); and Sidney Lanier succumbed to tuberculosis at a retreat in Polk County (1881).

**37**

1924.

**38**

Quakers.

**39**

False. Barbecue Presbyterian is a real church, established in 1757 in Harnett County. It took its name from nearby Barbecue Swamp, the mists from which reminded Scottish explorer Red Neill McNeill of smoke from barbecue pits he had seen in the West Indies.

**40**

The cigar in his hand.

**41**

Wilson, after the city's Appearance Commission recommended outlawing a longstanding southern custom: the use of upholstered furniture on porches.

**42**

Scrapple. The basic ingredients – hog's head, liver, and cornmeal – are the same.

**43**

"Keeping up with the Joneses."

**44**

Banana pudding.

**45**

False. During Reconstruction, Gen. Dan Sickles refused to allow the governors to adjourn their meeting and thus delay their formal acceptance of new voter registration laws. James Orr then remarked to Jonathan Worth, "The governor of South Carolina feels constrained to say to the governor of North Carolina, that in these military cabinet counsels, there is a mighty long time between drinks."

# MUSIC AND ENTERTAINMENT

*This 18-year-old Johnston County girl goes to the movie capital this week to begin a career in acting. Metro-Goldwyn-Mayer has signed her up for a 7-year-contract and it's easy to understand why.*

*The* Smithfield Herald, *in 1941, sending Ava Gardner off to Hollywood*

*She is far from being the most beautiful babe in the Hollywoods (her mouth is a little too large). Her figure is not the best (she is a trifle skinny and by Hollywood standards her legs are only average). Certainly few people – least of all herself – claim that she is a good actress (though she likes to think of herself as a singer). Yet she seems to exude the kind of allure that sets the mysterious Geiger counters which measure glamor clicking like subway turnstiles.*

Time *magazine, in 1951, finding its cover girl's appeal less understandable than did the* Smithfield Herald

# QUESTIONS

**1**

What TV show introduced the character of Andy Taylor, sheriff of Mayberry, N.C.?

**2**

What 1958 movie shot in Asheville and Transylvania County became a staple at drive-ins across the South?

**3**

Match the annual event with its site:

| | |
|---|---|
| Collard Festival | Ayden |
| Woolly Worm Festival | Saluda |
| Coon Dog Day | Banner Elk |
| Shad Festival | Grifton |

**4**

In the 1971 Emmy-winning movie *Brian's Song,* what actor played Brian Piccolo, the former Wake Forest running back who died of cancer at age twenty-six?

**5**

On a 1964 cross-country road trip from New York to New Orleans to San Francisco, this twenty-two-year-old folk singer dropped in on Carl Sandburg at his home in Flat Rock and received a chilly reception. Who was he?

**6**

Who played the title role in *Carbine Williams,* the 1952 movie about the Cumberland County prison inmate who developed the M-1 rifle?

**7**

What Mary Chapin Carpenter hit grew out of her annual visits to the Outer Banks?

**8**

In the premier episode of *The Andy Griffith Show,* Andy Taylor held two jobs in addition to sheriff. What were they?

**9**

What musician nearly died in a 1973 crash on I-85 near Salisbury?

**10**

What college fad began at UNC–Chapel Hill in 1974?

**11**

This 1994 movie, both set and filmed in Graham County, won a best-actress Oscar nomination for Jodie Foster. What is it?

**12**

According to Mayberry deputy Barney Fife, "You go read any book you want on the subject of child discipline and you'll find every one of them is in favor of . . ." what?

**13**

What 1975 hit by country music's Statler Brothers longed for the days of a Charlotte-reared Western movie star?

**14**

What band helped launch the alternative rock movement with a debut album recorded in Charlotte in 1983?

**15**

Match the entertainer with the college he or she attended:

| | |
|---|---|
| John Tesh | North Carolina State University |
| Carroll O'Connor | UNC-Greensboro |
| Emmylou Harris | Wake Forest University |
| Jack Palance | UNC–Chapel Hill |

**16**

What farm animal is celebrated each September in Benson?

**17**

Although best known for his television series, Andy Griffith won applause from movie critics for his role in what 1957 drama: *A Tree Grows in Brooklyn; Come Back, Little Sheba; The Three Faces of Eve;* or *A Face in the Crowd?*

**18**

In the 1986 action-adventure movie *Raw Deal,* what actor was cast as a sheriff in rural North Carolina?

**19**

Kathryn Grayson, star of 1940s musicals, and Pam Grier, star of 1970s "blaxploitation" movies, were born in the same town. What is it?

## 20

What mishap befell drummer Charlie Watts during the Rolling Stones's 1965 stop in Charlotte?

## 21

Actress Debra Paget was crowned queen of Wilmington's annual Azalea Festival in 1959. Who emceed her coronation?

## 22

What timeless musical was set on the Mississippi River but researched entirely on the North Carolina coast?

## 23

In 1965 Charlotte's Carolina Theatre was recognized as the first in the country to show a movie whose cumulative audience exceeded the city's population. What was the movie?

## 24

How many times has Miss North Carolina gone on to become Miss America?

## 25

True or false: Sheriff Taylor never smoked on *The Andy Griffith Show.*

## 26

What role did Durham play in the birth of *Amos 'n' Andy?*

## 27

True or false: Jazz greats John Coltrane, Thelonius Monk, and Dizzy Gillespie all were born in North Carolina.

**28**

A character based on Fayetteville native Archie Graham played a central role in what 1989 movie?

**29**

Singer James Taylor was born where: Austin, Boston, or Chapel Hill?

**30**

How did Raleigh newspaperman Josephus Daniels come to be dubbed "the Johnny Appleseed of jazz"?

**31**

Match the TV personality with the place where he or she retired.

| | |
|---|---|
| Perry Como | Raleigh |
| Frances Bavier | Saluda |
| Buffalo Bob Smith | Siler City |
| Kate Smith | Flat Rock |

**32**

What 1868 murder case led to a Grammy ninety years later for the Kingston Trio?

**33**

Charlotte-born John Scott Trotter conducted the orchestra for the best-selling single ever recorded. What was it?

**34**

What melancholy country music classic grew out of a 1936 auto accident in Rockingham?

**35**

The so-called "horn-tootin' bill" passed by the 1943 legislature gave the state what national "first"?

**36**

What amateur pianist played "Home on the Range" with Arthur Smith and the Crackerjacks during a 1964 taping of their country music TV show?

**37**

What classic folk ballad includes the line "You've got to get her to Spencer on time"?

**38**

In what order did Ava Gardner marry bandleader Artie Shaw, actor Mickey Rooney, and singer Frank Sinatra?

**39**

In the final episode of what sitcom did the title character comment, "I'm not sure why, if we're shooting an old guy into space, it's John Glenn and not Jesse Helms"?

**40**

What political activist was billed as "an extra added attraction" in Salisbury's Fourth of July parade in 1907?

**41**

Frank Sinatra was seventy-eight when he gave his last performance in North Carolina. Was it at the State Fair in Raleigh, the Fish Camp Jam in Gastonia, or the Azalea Festival in Wilmington?

**42**

In *Days of Thunder,* filmed at Charlotte Motor Speedway, Tom Cruise plays a NASCAR driver. What character does Nicole Kidman play?

## 43

Match the event with the president who attended:

| | |
|---|---|
| World Golf Hall of Fame opening, Pinehurst | George Bush |
| Fourth of July celebration, Faith | Bill Clinton |
| 30th Mustang Anniversary celebration, Charlotte | Gerald Ford |
| Billy Graham Day, Charlotte | Richard Nixon |

## 44

What native of Dunn influenced generations of rock musicians, including Peter Townshend of The Who?

## 45

Of Lester Flatt and Earl Scruggs, the bluegrass duo best remembered for "Foggy Mountain Breakdown" and the theme from *The Beverly Hillbillies,* which one is a North Carolinian?

## 46

What was on the flip side of "What It Was, Was Football," Andy Griffith's 1953 comedy hit?

## 47

What town is home to the musical groups Squirrel Nut Zippers, Red Clay Ramblers, and Southern Culture on the Skids?

## 48

What Iredell County town hosted "the South's Woodstock"?

## 49

What is Mayberry's "sister city"?

**50**

Where did Annie Oakley make her final appearance with Buffalo Bill's Wild West show?

**51**

What dramatic gesture did Annie Oakley make on behalf of a tuberculosis sanatorium near Pinehurst?

**52**

Movie actor Brandon Lee, son of martial arts legend Bruce Lee, was fatally wounded while filming *The Crow* in a Wilmington studio in 1993. What happened?

**53**

If Stephen Foster had stuck with his original version of "Old Folks at Home," what North Carolina river would have become a household word?

**54**

Match the country singer with his or her hometown:

| | |
|---|---|
| Ronnie Milsap ("Smoky Mountain Rain") | Mount Airy |
| Donna Fargo ("Happiest Girl in the Whole U.S.A.") | Tabor City |
| Don Gibson ("I Can't Stop Loving You") | Robbinsville |
| Stonewall Jackson ("Waterloo") | Shelby |

**55**

What TV star had to ride in a car instead of on his horse during a 1957 appearance at Greensboro's Memorial Stadium?

## 56

*Three in the Attic,* a 1969 movie in which Yvette Mimieux and two other coeds hold Christopher Jones hostage for sex and psychological thrills, was shot in a women's dorm on what campus?

## 57

Match the pop singer with his hometown:

| | |
|---|---|
| Sammy Johns ("Chevy Van") | Winston-Salem |
| Clyde McPhatter ("A Lover's Question") | Belhaven |
| George Hamilton IV ("A Rose and a Baby Ruth") | Charlotte |
| George Clinton ("One Nation Under a Groove") | Kannapolis |
| Little Eva ("The Loco-Motion") | Durham |

## 58

What entertainers were born Milton Supman, Richard Fliehr, and Randy Traywick?

## 59

The scene in the 1990 movie *The Hunt for Red October* in which the Soviet submarine glides into a Maine inlet was actually shot where?

## 60

In the 1964 rock 'n' roll hit "Promised Land," Chuck Berry says that on his trip home he did which of the following: "stopped at Charlotte but bypassed Rock Hill"; "stopped at Raleigh but bypassed Cary"; "stopped at Fayetteville but bypassed Lumberton"; or "stopped at Fuquay but bypassed Varina"?

**61**

*Rolling Stone* magazine praised this 1986 movie, filmed and set in Lumberton, as "an American masterpiece – surely the most audaciously original feature film made in this country in any recent year." What was it?

**62**

What Grammy-winning singer was elected to the Durham City Council in 1987?

**63**

Before going on to other careers, actor Andy Griffith, singer Roberta Flack, and novelist Clyde Edgerton all taught in North Carolina high schools. Where?

**64**

*The Swan,* the first of many movies to be shot at Biltmore House, was the last for its star, who retired after this 1956 costume romance. Who was she?

**65**

Nina Simone, who became a star with her rendition of "I Love You, Porgy," was born in the same town where DuBose Heyward, author of *Porgy,* died. What's the town?

**66**

In *Billy Bathgate,* a 1991 gangster movie starring Dustin Hoffman, what North Carolina town stood in for Onondaga, N.Y.?

**67**

What is MerleFest?

**68**

Which of director Steven Spielberg's movies was filmed in North Carolina?

**69**

Where was Barney Fife's favorite vacation spot?

**70**

What actress played Tiger Lily in East Carolina University's 1985 production of *Peter Pan?*

**71**

Which of these actors appeared briefly in two episodes of *The Andy Griffith Show:* Jack Nicholson, James Earl Jones, or Harrison Ford?

**72**

Rev. Joseph Chambers of Charlotte attracted national attention in 1993 when he attacked what TV character as "the leader of a children's cult"?

**73**

What 1987 movie was set at a Catskill Mountains resort but filmed at the Lake Lure Inn in Rutherford County?

**74**

By what stage name did Wilkes County native Bill Swofford achieve fame?

**75**

What action-adventure star was sued for accidentally injuring a stunt man during the 1988 filming of *Cyborg* in Wilmington?

**76**

*Thistle and Shamrock,* National Public Radio's Celtic music program, was first broadcast on what station?

**77**

After scouring the nation for an old-growth forest that could double as upstate New York in 1757, the director of the 1992 movie *The Last of the Mohicans* settled on a site on Lake James. How old were the trees there?

**78**

How many times did Gomer Pyle say "Golllly!" on *The Andy Griffith Show?*

**79**

What musical experience do politicians Jim Martin and Jesse Helms have in common?

**80**

What TV talk show host sued unsuccessfully to videotape and broadcast the 1994 execution of murderer David Lawson?

**81**

What actress won an Oscar in 1979 for her performance in *Norma Rae,* based on the union-organizing efforts of a real-life Roanoke Rapids textile worker?

**82**

What long-running rock group made its North Carolina debut in 1971 at Duke University's Wallace Wade Stadium?

**83**

What character on *The Andy Griffith Show* was notorious for throwing rocks through windows?

**84**

What black comedian was born Loretta Aiken in Brevard?

**85**

Bryan "Chainsaw Ted" Williams of Cherryville made his national debut on *The Tonight Show* in 1990. What was his act?

**86**

What popular TV series perpetuated the myth that Dr. Charles Drew, the black physician who helped set up the first American Red Cross blood bank, died after being refused treatment at Alamance General Hospital's emergency room?

**87**

What musician cut his first record in a Charlotte warehouse in 1936?

**88**

What singer made a bow to the regional culture by telling her Charlotte audience in 1994, "It was either us or a monster truck show"?

**89**

What 1972 movie appropriated Charlotte musician Arthur Smith's 1950s hit "Feudin' Banjos," renamed it "Dueling Banjos," and used it without credit or payment?

**90**

In what song do these lines appear: "Tho' the scorner may sneer at and witlings defame her, / Still our hearts swell with gladness whenever we name her"?

**91**

What performer gave his first Charlotte performance at the Carolina Theatre in 1956 on a bill with Mother Maybelle and the Carter Sisters?

## 92

What late-night comedian characterized Sen. Jesse Helms as "the kind of guy who would jump in his pickup truck and try to run over Forrest Gump"?

## 93

What actress, appearing in Raleigh in a 1941 stage version of *The Philadelphia Story,* told reporters she hadn't seen enough of North Carolina to form an opinion, "but the beds in the hotel are nice"?

## 94

What provoked country musician Charlie Daniels to call two student newspaper columnists at UNC-Wilmington "pea-brained intellectuals" and "fledgling bigots"?

## 95

In what 1993 movie did a TVA dam in Graham County play a key part?

## 96

Don Knotts won five Emmys for playing Barney Fife on *The Andy Griffith Show.* How many did Griffith win?

# ANSWERS

**1**

*The Danny Thomas Show.* In a 1960 episode,
Sheriff Taylor, played by Andy Griffith, arrested
nightclub performer Thomas for speeding
through his sleepy town. Thus was set up television's first spinoff series, *The Andy Griffith
Show.*

**2**

*Thunder Road.* Robert Mitchum starred as a
moonshiner and even recorded the title song.

**3**

Collard Festival, Ayden; Woolly Worm Festival, Banner Elk; Coon Dog Day, Saluda; Shad
Festival, Grifton.

**4**

James Caan. Billy Dee Williams played Gale
Sayers, Piccolo's roommate with the Chicago
Bears.

**5**

Bob Dylan. Sandburg thought Dylan was full of
himself.

**6**

Jimmy Stewart.

**7**

"I Am a Town." ("I'm a town in Carolina, I'm a detour on a ride / For a phone call and a soda, I'm a blur from the driver's side.")

**8**

Justice of the peace and newspaper editor.

**9**

Stevie Wonder, who suffered a brain contusion and spent two weeks in Baptist Hospital in Winston-Salem. (His only long-term impairment: loss of his sense of smell.)

**10**

Streaking. On March 5, more than two hundred male students stripped bare and raced across the campus and through the undergraduate library. Twenty women from Joyner Dormitory joined in. Two days later, to accompaniment by the university's pep band, more than nine hundred naked students ran single-file through an appreciative crowd before posing for a group photo near South Building. Streaking quickly spread to campuses across the nation before the fad abruptly expired.

**11**

*Nell,* in which Foster plays an isolated mountain woman who speaks a self-created language.

**12**

"Bud nipping." "Nip it in the bud" (or "nip it") was one of Fife's favorite expressions, being used in at least six episodes of *The Andy Griffith Show.*

**13**

"Whatever Happened to Randolph Scott?"
Sample lyric: "Whatever happened to Randolph Scott, riding the range alone? / Whatever happened to Gene and Roy, gee, I'd like to know."

**14**

R.E.M. The band from Athens, Georgia, cut "Murmur" at Reflection Studios.

**15**

John Tesh, N.C. State; Carroll O'Connor, Wake Forest; Emmylou Harris, UNC-Greensboro; Jack Palance, UNC–Chapel Hill.

**16**

The mule. Until the tractor took over after World War II, the mule was the foundation of agriculture in such eastern North Carolina communities as Benson, which began its annual Mule Days in 1950.

**17**

*A Face in the Crowd.*

**18**

Arnold Schwarzenegger. (His most memorable line, delivered after his inebriated wife has just missed him with a cake: "You should not drink and bake.")

**19**

Winston-Salem.

**20**

According to a memoir by bass player Bill Wyman, Watts and a photographer were "beaten up in the hotel coffee bar by a little old lady with an umbrella, who looked exactly like

Granny Clampett of 'The Beverly Hillbillies.'
She'd taken a dislike to them because of the
length of their hair. The manager finally led her
away."

**21**

Ronald Reagan, then host of TV's *General
Electric Theater.*

**22**

*Show Boat.* In 1925 Edna Ferber spent several days aboard the *James Adams Floating
Theatre,* a showboat making a stop at Bath.

**23**

*The Sound of Music.* Total attendance was
247,000; Charlotte's estimated population was
238,000.

**24**

Once. Maria Beale Fletcher of Asheville won in
1961.

**25**

False. He lit up in at least ten episodes, almost
all aired before the surgeon general's report of
1964 that linked smoking with cancer.

**26**

That's where Charles Correll and Freeman
Gosden, brought in separately to produce an
Elks follies in 1920, began a collaboration that
would result in perhaps the most popular radio
show of all time.

**27**

False. Coltrane was born in Hamlet, Monk
in Rocky Mount, and Gillespie in Cheraw,
South Carolina (although he graduated from
Laurinburg Institute in Scotland County).

**28**

*Field of Dreams.* Like his fictional counterpart, the real-life "Moonlight" Graham, older brother of academician Frank Porter Graham, played only a half-inning in the major leagues before going on to medical school and a long career as a small-town Minnesota physician.

**29**

Boston. He grew up in Chapel Hill, where his father was dean of the UNC medical school.

**30**

During his tenure as secretary of the navy during World War I, Daniels acted to clean up the red-light districts that fed off sailors. When he declared New Orleans's Storyville off-limits, Daniels removed the economic base of the early jazz musicians, causing them to scatter to Chicago, Kansas City, and St. Louis.

**31**

Perry Como, Saluda; Frances Bavier, Siler City; Buffalo Bob Smith, Flat Rock; Kate Smith, Raleigh.

**32**

Tom Dula's stabbing of his pregnant girlfriend, Laura Foster. Even before Dula was convicted and hanged, a ballad was being sung in Wilkes and Watauga Counties. The Kingston Trio successfully revived "Tom Dooley" in 1958.

**33**

Bing Crosby's 1942 rendition of Irving Berlin's "White Christmas." It sold more than thirty million copies.

**34**

"The Wreck on the Highway," first recorded in
Charlotte by its composers, Dorsey and Howard
Dixon, but made famous by Roy Acuff.

**35**

First state to provide continuing financial
support for an orchestra – the North Carolina
Symphony.

**36**

Former vice president Richard Nixon, making
a "nonpolitical" tour of the state between
campaigns.

**37**

"The Wreck of Old 97." Spencer was the half-
way point between Southern Railway's twin
headquarters in Washington and Atlanta. Old
97 failed to make it to Spencer at all, having
wrecked in Danville, Va., but the engine was
brought there for repairs.

**38**

Rooney, Shaw, Sinatra.

**39**

*Murphy Brown.*

**40**

Carry Nation. After inspecting the town's
saloons, she pronounced it a "hell hole."

**41**

The Azalea Festival, in 1994.

**42**

A brain surgeon.

**43**

World Golf Hall of Fame, Gerald Ford; Fourth of July, George Bush; 30th Mustang Anniversary, Bill Clinton; Billy Graham Day, Richard Nixon.

**44**

Link Wray, whose 1958 instrumental "Rumble" introduced fuzz-tone guitar distortion. "If it hadn't been for Link Wray and 'Rumble,'" Townshend has said, "I would never have picked up a guitar."

**45**

Banjo player Scruggs, who is from Cleveland County.

**46**

Griffith's southern-style "Romeo and Juliet." (When Juliet asks, "Wherefore art thou, Romeo?" Romeo pops up from behind a bush and responds, "Ah'm raight cheer!")

**47**

Chapel Hill–Carrboro.

**48**

Love Valley, in 1970. The three-day Love Valley Rock Festival, headlined by the Allman Brothers, attracted a crowd estimated at 75,000.

**49**

Mount Pilot. (The likely source of the town's name, Pilot Mountain, is situated near Andy Griffith's hometown of Mount Airy.)

**50**

Charlotte, in 1901. The troupe had played to a crowd of 12,000 at Latta Park and was en route to Danville, Virginia, when its train collided head-on with a southbound freight near Linwood in Davidson County. The show didn't resume for another year, and by then Oakley had gone out on her own.

## 51

She had her twenty-seven shooting medals melted down, then donated the gold. Oakley and her husband, Frank Butler, spent several winters teaching and entertaining guests at the Carolina Hotel in Pinehurst.

## 52

He was shot by a prop gun that was supposed to contain blank cartridges. Instead, the tip of a real bullet had become lodged in the chamber during filming of an earlier scene. Lee, twenty-eight, bled to death.

## 53

The Pee Dee. Foster initially wrote, "Way down upon the Pedee ribber," but for reasons unknown scratched out "Pedee" and inserted "Swanee." The Pee Dee is formed in Montgomery County at the junction of the Yadkin and Uwharrie Rivers and continues on to the South Carolina coast.

## 54

Milsap, Robbinsville; Fargo, Mount Airy; Gibson, Shelby; Jackson, Tabor City.

## 55

Clayton Moore, the Lone Ranger, after Silver threw him the previous night in Asheville. Moore, who was treated for a sprained knee and chipped elbow, walked on crutches but still managed to put on a quick-draw exhibition.

**56**

UNC–Chapel Hill.

**57**

Johns, Charlotte; McPhatter, Durham; Hamilton, Winston-Salem; Clinton, Kannapolis; Little Eva (Boyd), Belhaven.

**58**

Supman, a Franklinton native, became comedian Soupy Sales; Fliehr, a longtime Charlotte resident, became wrestler Ric Flair; and Traywick, a Marshville native, is known today as country singer Randy Travis.

**59**

Lake James on the Catawba River in Burke and McDowell Counties. (Turnabout: The 1999 romance *Message in a Bottle* was set on the Outer Banks but filmed in Maine.)

**60**

He "stopped at Charlotte but bypassed Rock Hill."

**61**

*Blue Velvet,* directed by David Lynch.

**62**

Shirley Caesar, winner of nine Grammy Awards and a member of the Gospel Music Hall of Fame.

**63**

Griffith in Goldsboro, Flack in Farmville, Edgerton in Durham.

**64**

Grace Kelly.

**65**

Tryon.

**66**

Hamlet.

**67**

An annual festival founded by Doc Watson to honor his son and musical collaborator, Merle, who died in a tractor accident. Since 1988 MerleFest has attracted to Wilkesboro such musicians as Emmylou Harris, Chet Atkins, Earl Scruggs, Ricky Skaggs, Alison Krauss, Guy Clark, and Arlo Guthrie.

**68**

*The Color Purple* (1985), in Marshville.

**69**

The Raleigh YMCA ("corner room").

**70**

Sandra Bullock, future star of *Speed* and *While You Were Sleeping*. She also waited on tables at a Darryl's Restaurant before leaving ECU for New York after her junior year.

**71**

Jack Nicholson. He played a husband who abandons a baby in one episode, a burglar on trial in the other.

**72**

Barney, the purple dinosaur. According to Chambers's tract "The Purple Messiah," "Barney teaches a host of different things, but nothing comes through louder than the New Age idea of using our minds to create miracles. . . . Protect your children and family with your life!"

**73**

*Dirty Dancing,* starring Patrick Swayze.

**74**

Oliver, best known for the 1970s pop hits "Jean" and "Good Morning Starshine." He's also the older brother of John Swofford, executive director of the Atlantic Coast Conference and former athletic director at UNC–Chapel Hill.

**75**

Jean-Claude Van Damme. A jury awarded $487,500 to Jackson "Rock" Pinckney, who lost the sight in his left eye after being cut by a prop knife during a fight scene with Van Damme.

**76**

WFAE at UNC-Charlotte, where Scottish-born Fiona Ritchie was a teaching assistant in the psychology department during the early 1980s.

**77**

Between nineteen and thirty years old. Crescent Resources, a Duke Power subsidiary, had clear-cut and replanted the pines.

**78**

Only once, on May 19, 1964. "Golllly!" became a catchword, however, on Jim Nabors's spinoff show, *Gomer Pyle, U.S.M.C.*

**79**

Each played tuba in his high school band.

**80**

Phil Donahue. The U.S. Supreme Court rejected his request, and Lawson's death in the gas chamber at Central Prison in Raleigh went untelevised.

**81**

Sally Field.

**82**

The Grateful Dead. Not yet a cult phenomenon, the Dead shared a "Joe College Weekend" bill with the Paul Butterfield Blues Band and the Beach Boys.

**83**

Ernest T. Bass.

**84**

Jackie "Moms" Mabley, whose career stretched from vaudeville to *The Smothers Brothers Comedy Hour.* She died in 1975.

**85**

He imitated the sounds made by a chainsaw, motorcycles, and (with his head in a bucket of water) an outboard motor.

**86**

*M*A*S*H.* According to both Drew's widow and another black doctor who was at the hospital, white doctors made every effort to save Drew's life after an auto accident near Burlington in 1950.

**87**

Bill Monroe, future father of bluegrass music. It was during six Charlotte sessions over the next two years that Monroe won acceptance for the mandolin as a lead instrument in country music.

**88**

Bette Midler.

**89**

*Deliverance.* Warner Bros. eventually paid Smith an estimated $200,000 in an out-of-court settlement.

**90**

"The Old North State," composed in 1840 by state supreme court justice William Gaston and designated in 1927 as the official state song.

**91**

Elvis Presley, eighteen years old and only days away from being introduced to the nation on the Tommy Dorsey and Ed Sullivan TV shows.

**92**

David Letterman.

**93**

Katharine Hepburn.

**94**

They questioned his fitness to be the school's 1996 commencement speaker.

**95**

*The Fugitive.* Dr. Richard Kimble, played by Harrison Ford, jumps off the dam to escape his pursuers.

**96**

None.

# SPORTS AND RECREATION

*A grand cock-fight between North Carolina and South Carolina birds might better have been omitted from the programme.*

Harper's Weekly, *reviewing the centennial celebration of the Mecklenburg Declaration of Independence in Charlotte in 1875*

*I tried to get the Chamber of Commerce involved, but one of them said, "Hell, he buys his tractors in Greenville."*

Dr. Martel Dailey of Williamston, *lamenting the failure of Gaylord Perry's hometown to honor him after he won his second Cy Young Award in 1978*

# QUESTIONS

**1**

What North Carolina town is named for a member of the Baseball Hall of Fame?

**2**

A UNC–Chapel Hill basketball star of the 1990s shares his name with Gomer Pyle's drill instructor. What is it?

**3**

When potential visitors to North Carolina call 1-800-VISITNC for information, who answers the phone?

**4**

The first player ever cut from the Carolina Panthers roster went on to achieve top billing in another arena. Who is he?

**5**

At his induction into the Baseball Hall of Fame in 1978, he told the audience, "I guess I began my career at age eleven, when I was a batboy for the Greensboro Patriots." Who was he?

**6**

Rival street gangs in what city have adopted the sports apparel of UNC–Chapel Hill and Duke?

**7**

Match the baseball star with his minor league team:

| | |
|---|---|
| Cal Ripken | Gastonia Rangers |
| Sammy Sosa | Raleigh Caps |
| Don Mattingly | Charlotte O's |
| Carl Yastrzemski | Greensboro Hornets |

**8**

"God created the golf course. I uncover it." What esteemed course designer summarized his philosophy in these words?

**9**

In 1999 the Charlotte Hornets gave a tryout to what rap star: Master P, Ice Cube, or Puffy Combs?

**10**

Why did the N.C. General Assembly declare Easter Monday a state holiday in 1935? And why did it change the holiday to Good Friday in 1987?

**11**

Which one of these is not a native North Carolinian: Crystal Lee Jordan (later Sutton), the mill worker who inspired the movie *Norma Rae;* B. Everett Jordan, Jesse Helms's predecessor in the U.S. Senate; Michael Jordan, basketball player; or Hamilton Jordan, aide to President Jimmy Carter?

**12**

What was North Carolina's first ski resort?

**13**

In 1991 Florida State guard Sam Cassell, finding fans in UNC–Chapel Hill's Smith Center considerably less rowdy than those at Duke's Cameron Indoor Stadium, stuck them with what memorable label?

**14**

Name the elective offices held by former major league pitchers Wilmer "Vinegar Bend" Mizell, Ernie Shore, and Tommy Byrne.

**15**

The state's first recognized intercollegiate football game was played in what year: 1888, 1898, or 1908?

**16**

What part in Olympic history was played by the Rocky Mount Railroaders?

**17**

What North Carolina athlete, described as looking "a little like Rudolph Valentino made up as Superman," made the cover of *Life* magazine in 1949?

**18**

Identify these North Carolina sports figures: Catfish, Cornbread, Peahead, Meadowlark, and Bighouse.

**19**

What future legend almost became Duke's head basketball coach in 1949?

**20**

What past legend almost became Duke's head basketball coach in 1972?

**21**

Harry Gant of Taylorsville is the oldest driver ever to win a Winston Cup stock-car race. Was he forty-two, fifty-two, or sixty-two years old?

**22**

True or false: In 1957 North Carolina captured its first NCAA basketball tournament championship by winning back-to-back double-overtime games.

**23**

What golfer, on his way to a record eleven straight PGA tour victories, won the Charlotte Open, Greensboro Open, and Durham Open on successive weekends?

**24**

In a 1979 game at Cameron Indoor Stadium, a badly missed shot by Rich Yonakor of North Carolina provoked what innovative response from Duke fans?

**25**

A 1964 basketball game for the high school championship of Harnett County is the longest ever played in high school, college, or professional competition. How many overtimes did it take Boone Trail to defeat Angier, 56–54?

**26**

Where was the Rose Bowl played in 1942?

**27**

One theory says that baseball's "bullpen" is an outgrowth of a term used for an enclosure to hold prisoners. What's the other theory?

**28**

Which heavyweight champion died in Raleigh?
Which one was born in Cleveland County?
Which one sang the national anthem at Charlotte Motor Speedway? Which one trained
outside Hendersonville before losing his title
to Gene Tunney? Which one went to jail for
kidnapping his estranged wife from Cornelius?
Which one graduated from Shaw University?

**29**

What demonstrative Wake Forest basketball
coach strapped himself to his chair on the
sidelines to restrain himself from committing
technical fouls?

**30**

After suffering facial cuts in a 1974 crash
at Charlotte Motor Speedway, what driver
ordered the ambulance crew to make sure a
plastic surgeon was standing by at the hospital?

**31**

What event do the state's ACC basketball fans
remember as "Black Sunday"?

**32**

True or false: Crash Davis, Kevin Costner's
character in *Bull Durham,* was a real baseball
player.

**33**

Which of North Carolina's major league sports
teams was almost named "Spirit"?

**34**

What was the Dixie Classic?

**35**

A rare fashion flop for Chapel Hill's Alexander Julian was the uniform he designed for the Charlotte Knights minor-league baseball team in 1990. What color was it?

**36**

The annual Textile Bowl matches football teams from what two colleges?

**37**

In the decades after the Civil War, why did wealthy northerners buy up thousands of acres on Currituck Sound?

**38**

Which of these nicknames has *not* been widely attached to NASCAR driver Dale Earnhardt: Man in Black, Intimidator, Ironhead, or Air Dale?

**39**

When basketball coach Everett Case arrived at North Carolina State University in 1946, what victory ritual did he bring with him from Indiana high schools?

**40**

What untraditional accomplishment won Francis Rogallo of Kitty Hawk a place in the North Carolina Sports Hall of Fame?

**41**

The outbreak of World War II moved this freshman football player to quit UNC–Chapel Hill for the military, but he still went on to win a Heisman Trophy. Who was he?

## 42

What place in basketball history is held by Ronnie Carr of Western Carolina University?

## 43

What baseball great made his debut with the amateur Murphy Maulers?

## 44

What mountain town of 2,100 once held a franchise in the Atlantic Coast Hockey League?

## 45

The Carolina Cougars of the American Basketball Association grew out of an idea put forth by what renowned sportswriter?

## 46

Which, if any, of these events has *not* been part of a pre-race show at Charlotte Motor Speedway (now Lowe's Motor Speedway): A reenactment of the U.S. military invasion of Grenada; an appearance by Elizabeth Taylor as grand marshal; a mock *Dukes of Hazzard* chase scene; a Barney Fife impersonator doing the macarena; or a stunt driver in a Winnebago jumping over "the world's biggest outhouse," which has just exploded?

## 47

George Glamack, a two-time All America basketball player at the University of North Carolina in the 1940s, had such bad eyesight that he was nicknamed what?

## 48

In 1950 North Carolina led the nation in its number of minor-league baseball teams. How many teams did it field: fifteen, twenty-five, or forty-five?

**49**

Match these members of the Baseball Hall of Fame with their hometowns:

Luke Appling    Rocky Mount
Buck Leonard    Williamston
Gaylord Perry    High Point
Hoyt Wilhelm    Huntersville

**50**

Who are Lee, Richard, Kyle, and Adam?

**51**

How many teams had Dean Smith taken to the Final Four before the Tar Heels beat Georgetown to win the national championship in 1982?

**52**

The athletic teams of what college are known as the Fightin' Christians?

**53**

Luther "Wimpy" Lassiter of Elizabeth City is the lone representative of his sport in the North Carolina Sports Hall of Fame. What is it?

**54**

Who made stock car racing's "pass in the grass"?

**55**

What fish has begun appearing in great numbers off Cape Hatteras each winter?

**56**

What do crawdads, boll weevils, and warthogs have in common?

**57**

UNC–Chapel Hill forward Bobby Jones played on the 1972 Olympic basketball team but has no medal to show for it. Why not?

**58**

What racial breakthrough did C. B. Claiborne achieve in 1965?

**59**

What celebrity golf tournament moved to Bermuda Run Country Club near Winston-Salem in 1986?

**60**

The career of Shelby-born basketball legend David Thompson was cut short by a knee injury. How did it happen?

**61**

What major fad of the 1920s originated in Pinehurst?

**62**

N.C. State's basketball team went 27–0 in 1972–73 but failed to win the national championship. Why?

**63**

What Charlotte native was known as "golf's Jackie Robinson"?

**64**

Who came down with "the bellyache heard 'round the world"?

**65**

Who was the first African American to play in an integrated baseball game at McCormick Field in Asheville?

## 66

How was the winning basket made in underdog N.C. State's 54–52 victory over Houston in the 1983 NCAA championship game?

## 67

In a 1948 game at N.C. State, Yale's first baseman went three for four with a triple, double, three RBIs, two runs scored, a sacrifice, and a stolen base. Who was he?

## 68

What world-renowned sportscaster was born in Winston-Salem?

## 69

Carowinds, the Carolinas' first major theme park, opened on the South Carolina border near Charlotte in what year: 1953, 1963, or 1973?

## 70

The first Charlotte Speedway, built in the 1920s, had what surface?

## 71

What baseball great hit a home run in the first game played at Asheville's McCormick Field?

## 72

What basketball coach was burned in effigy on campus after a 1965 loss to Wake Forest?

## 73

What stock-car driver was paid homage by both Tom Wolfe, in *The Last American Hero*, and Bruce Springsteen, in "Cadillac Ranch"?

# ANSWERS

**1**

Landis, in Rowan County. In 1907 Kennesaw Mountain Landis, a federal judge in Illinois, made headlines by fining Standard Oil $29 million for monopolistic trade practices, after which the fledgling town named itself after him. In 1920, in the wake of the Black Sox scandal, Landis was chosen the first commissioner of baseball.

**2**

Vince Carter. Sergeant Carter (played by Frank Sutton) was introduced on the 1964 episode of *The Andy Griffith Show* that served as the pilot for *Gomer Pyle, U.S.M.C.*

**3**

A prisoner at the N.C. Correctional Institution for Women. The program, begun in 1989, is overseen by the state's Travel and Tourism Division.

**4**

Journeyman tackle Bill Goldberg, who found fame as simply "Goldberg" in World Championship Wrestling.

**5**

Mel Allen, longtime "Voice of the Yankees."

**6**

Chicago. The Maniac Latin Disciples wear the colors of UNC, the Gangster Disciples those of Duke.

**7**

Ripken, Charlotte O's; Sosa, Gastonia Rangers; Mattingly, Greensboro Hornets; Yastrzemski, Raleigh Caps.

**8**

Scottish-born Donald Ross, who arrived in Pinehurst in 1900 and spent forty-eight years there, laying out the revered Pinehurst No. 2 – site of the 1999 U.S. Open – and hundreds of other courses across the country. Today the Sandhills region boasts of having more golf courses per square mile than any other place in the world.

**9**

Master P (real name, Percy Miller) was cut in training camp, but not before almost single-handedly drawing 15,000 fans to an intrasquad scrimmage. Ranked by *Forbes Magazine* as the nation's tenth-highest-paid entertainer, Miller played guard in college and in the Continental Basketball Association.

**10**

It designated Easter Monday to accommodate state employees who wanted to attend the annual baseball game between cross-county rivals N.C. State and Wake Forest (then actually located in the town of Wake Forest). It switched to Good Friday to accommodate banks, which had complained about being out of step with the rest of the nation.

**11**

Michael Jordan, who grew up in Wilmington but was born in New York City. (Hamilton Jordan was born in Charlotte.)

**12**

Cataloochee Ski Ranch in Haywood County, which opened in 1961.

**13**

"A cheese-and-wine crowd."

**14**

Mizell was U.S. Congressman from Winston-Salem; Shore was sheriff of Forysth County, and Byrne was mayor of Wake Forest.

**15**

1888. Wake Forest defeated the University of North Carolina, 6–4, in Raleigh.

**16**

Jim Thorpe had to return his gold medals from the 1912 Olympics after it was revealed he had been paid $2 a game during a brief stint with the Railroaders, a semipro baseball team. The medals were restored in 1982.

**17**

UNC–Chapel Hill halfback Charlie "Choo Choo" Justice.

**18**

Jim "Catfish" Hunter, baseball pitcher from Hertford; Cedric "Cornbread" Maxwell, basketball player from Kinston and UNC-Charlotte; Clarence "Peahead" Walker, football coach at Wake Forest; George "Meadowlark" Lemon, Harlem Globetrotter from Wilmington;

Clarence "Bighouse" Gaines, basketball coach at Winston-Salem State.

**19**

Red Auerbach, who left Duke for the NBA after three months as assistant and designated successor to the fatally ill Jerry Gerard.

**20**

Adolph Rupp, who accepted the Duke job, then rejected it, after being forced to retire from the University of Kentucky.

**21**

Fifty-two.

**22**

False. They were back-to-back triple-overtime games.

**23**

Byron Nelson, in 1945.

**24**

"Airrrr balllll." The taunt soon became a staple in basketball arenas across the country.

**25**

Thirteen.

**26**

In Durham, out of fear the Japanese would bomb Pasadena, California. The University of Oregon upset previously undefeated Duke, 20–16.

**27**

That it stems from pitchers warming up beneath the Bull Durham billboard in the outfield.

**28**

Jack Johnson (at age seventy, from injuries suffered in a car crash), Floyd Patterson, Joe Frazier, Jack Dempsey, Riddick Bowe, James "Bonecrusher" Smith.

**29**

Horace "Bones" McKinney, later coach of the American Basketball Association's Carolina Cougars and announcer at ACC basketball games. "I plead guilty," McKinney wrote in his 1988 autobiography, "to driving through life at about 80 miles an hour, drinking 60,000 Pepsi-Colas, smoking some 2 million cigarettes and threatening the lives of several hundred referees."

**30**

Marty Robbins, better known for such country-and-western hits as "El Paso."

**31**

On March 11, 1979, St. John's and the University of Pennsylvania came to Raleigh and posted two of the biggest upsets in the history of the NCAA tournament. St. John's, the fortieth and last team selected, beat No. 2 seed Duke, and Penn of the Ivy League came from behind to beat No. 1 seed North Carolina.

**32**

True. Lawrence "Crash" Davis, a Gastonia native, played for the Durham Bulls in 1948. Writer-director Ron Shelton happened onto Davis's name while thumbing through a Carolina League record book and claimed it for his lead character.

**33**

Basketball's Charlotte Hornets. Spirit was the choice of the franchise's advisory board, but a later name-the-team contest ranked Hornets first and Spirit a distant fourth.

**34**

College basketball's first Christmas holiday tournament, founded in 1949. Held at Reynolds Coliseum in Raleigh, it matched the Big Four – N.C. State, UNC–Chapel Hill, Duke, and Wake Forest – against four out-of-state powers. The point-shaving scandal of 1960–61 caused State and UNC to deemphasize basketball, and the Dixie Classic was among the casualties.

**35**

Black, with stripes of thirteen different colors. Julian's design, panned in *Sports Illustrated* as "Knightmarish," was ditched after one year.

**36**

N.C. State and Clemson.

**37**

To establish hunting clubs, from which members could take advantage of Currituck's proliferation of ducks each winter.

**38**

Air Dale.

**39**

Cutting down the nets after tournament championship games.

**40**

Rogallo, a NASA scientist, invented the flexible-wing hang glider.

**41**

Felix "Doc" Blanchard. Playing for Army, Blanchard and Glenn Davis became known as Mr. Inside and Mr. Outside, perhaps the most famous running duo in the history of college football.

**42**

In a 1980 game against Middle Tennessee State, Carr hit college basketball's first three-point goal. The Southern Conference had won approval to score three points for shots taken outside a twenty-two-foot semicircle, but it would be 1986 before the rule went into effect for all NCAA games.

**43**

Ty Cobb. At home in Royston, Georgia, Ty's father – a teacher and graduate of North Carolina Agricultural College – prohibited ball playing. But during Ty's summer visits to his grandfather's farm near Murphy, he got his first taste of "town ball."

**44**

Spruce Pine, home of the Pinebridge Bucks during the 1980s.

**45**

Frank Deford, who had proposed in *Sports Illustrated* that a regional franchise, rather than a traditional one based in a single city, would flourish in basketball-mad North Carolina. The Cougars were headquartered in Greensboro during their five seasons in the early 1970s but also played in Charlotte and Raleigh.

**46**

All have happened.

**47**

"The Blind Bomber."

**48**

Forty-five. By 1998, the number had fallen to eleven (including the Charlotte Knights, who play across the border in South Carolina).

**49**

Appling, High Point; Leonard, Rocky Mount; Perry, Williamston; Wilhelm, Huntersville.

**50**

Four generations of stock car racing's first family – the Pettys of Randleman.

**51**

Six.

**52**

Elon College.

**53**

Pool. Lassiter, who died in 1988, was considered by some to be the greatest nine-ball player ever.

**54**

Dale Earnhardt, after Bill Elliott forced him into the infield grass while racing for the lead in the 1987 Winston at Charlotte Motor Speedway. Earnhardt turned near-calamity into a piece of history by maintaining control, returning to the asphalt in the lead, and winning the race.

**55**

The bluefin tuna. Fishermen are ecstatic, scientists baffled.

**56**

All have minor-league baseball teams named after them, in Hickory, Kannapolis, and Winston-Salem, respectively.

**57**

The United States, undefeated since basketball's debut as an Olympic sport, lost 51–50 to the Soviet Union in a fiercely disputed gold-medal game at Munich. Along with his eleven teammates, Jones refused his silver medal, which remains in a Swiss vault.

**58**

As a reserve for Duke, he became the first black ACC basketball player for a North Carolina school. A year before, Maryland's Billy Jones and Pete Johnson had become the league's first black players, and a year later Charlie Scott at North Carolina would become its first black star.

**59**

The Crosby. The Bing Crosby Pro-Am had been held in Pebble Beach, California, since 1937, but Crosby's widow, Kathryn, relocated it after a dispute with sponsors.

**60**

In 1983, while a player for the Seattle Super-Sonics, he fell down a flight of stairs at Studio 54, a New York disco.

**61**

Miniature golf. In 1916 James Barber, looking for a way to entertain houseguests, laid out the game's first course in the garden of his estate. Barber's idea lay commercially dormant for a decade, until two New York promoters built a course atop a skyscraper in hopes of attracting Wall Streeters on their lunch breaks. By 1930 Americans were playing at some 23,000 miniature golf courses nationwide. The industry leader today is the Fayetteville-based Putt-Putt chain.

**62**

The school was on NCAA probation for recruiting violations and was therefore barred from tournament play.

**63**

Charlie Sifford, who became the first black player on the PGA tour after its "Caucasians only" clause was stricken in 1961.

**64**

Babe Ruth, who was stricken with an intestinal abscess as the New York Yankees arrived in Asheville for a 1925 exhibition game. When Ruth's arrival back in New York was delayed, rumors of his death spread. (That false report was quickly squelched, but the one attributing his attack to gorging on hot dogs became part of the Ruthian legend.)

**65**

Jackie Robinson, who went hitless against the minor-league Asheville Tourists in a 1948 exhibition. The Brooklyn Dodgers had chosen Asheville as an exhibition site after canceling games in Atlanta and Jacksonville, Florida, out of fear of racial violence.

**66**

Lorenzo Charles turned teammate Dereck Whittenburg's too-short thirty-five-footer into a buzzer-beating slam dunk.

**67**

George Bush.

**68**

Howard Cosell. His father, an accountant for a credit clothing chain, happened to be living in Winston-Salem at the time. Later the family moved to Raleigh, then to Brooklyn, all before Howard turned three. "It is a piece of biographical data I now find curious," Cosell would write of his North Carolina roots.

**69**

1973.

**70**

Wooden planks.

**71**

Ty Cobb of the Detroit Tigers, in an exhibition game against the Asheville Skylanders in 1924. By 1991, when the stadium was razed, it had become the oldest minor-league park in the country.

**72**

Dean Smith, then in his fourth year at North Carolina.

**73**

Junior Johnson, the Wilkes County moonshine runner who went on to win fifty NASCAR races.